Philosophy of Love

Books by Irving Singer

Philosophy of Love: A Partial Summing-Up

Cinematic Mythmaking: Philosophy in Film

Meaning in Life trilogy with new prefaces, The Irving Singer Library

The Nature of Love trilogy with new prefaces, The Irving Singer Library

Ingmar Bergman, Cinematic Philosopher: Reflections on His Creativity

Three Philosophical Filmmakers: Hitchcock, Welles, Renoir

Sex: A Philosophical Primer, expanded edition

Feeling and Imagination: The Vibrant Flux of Our Existence

Sex: A Philosophical Primer

Explorations in Love and Sex

George Santayana, Literary Philosopher

Reality Transformed: Film as Meaning and Technique

Meaning in Life:
The Creation of Value
The Pursuit of Love
The Harmony of Nature and Spirit

The Nature of Love:
Plato to Luther
Courtly and Romantic
The Modern World

Mozart and Beethoven: The Concept of Love in Their Operas

The Goals of Human Sexuality

Santayana's Aesthetics

Essays in Literary Criticism by George Santayana (editor)

The Nature and Pursuit of Love: The Philosophy of Irving Singer (edited by David Goicoechea)

Philosophy of Love

A Partial Summing-Up

Irving Singer

The MIT Press
Cambridge, Massachusetts
London, England

For information about special quantity discounts, please email special_sales@mitpress.mit.edu.

This book was set in Palatino by SNP Best-set Typesetter Ltd., Hong Kong, and was printed and bound in the United States of America.

Library of Congress Cataloging-in-Publication Data

Singer, Irving.
Philosophy of love : a partial summing-up / Irving Singer.
    p. cm.—(The Irving Singer library)
Includes index.
ISBN 978-0-262-19574-4 (hardcover : alk. paper)   1. Love.   I. Title.
BD436.S522   2009
128'.46—dc22   2008035944

10 9 8 7 6 5 4 3 2 1

To the Society for the Philosophy of Sex and Love.
May it long endure!

Contents

Foreword

Alan Soble

In the early 1970s, while I was a graduate student in philosophy at the State University of New York at Buffalo, I read two things (both well outside my standard course of study) that had an enormous influence on my subsequent scholarly career.

One thing was Thomas Nagel's 1969 essay in the *Journal of Philosophy*, "Sexual Perversion," which showed me that a contemporary combination of analytic and continental philosophy could significantly illuminate human sexuality. I began to think that the philosophical investigation of sexuality could become a serious and respected branch of the philosophical tree.

The other thing was Irving Singer's *Plato to Luther*, the first edition (1966) of the first volume of his monumental trilogy *The Nature of Love*, which demonstrated to me how intricate and fascinating the philosophical

and historical scrutiny of the idea of love could be.
Looking back on the year 1977, it does not strike me as
surprising, more than three decades later, that I was
then provoked to establish the Society for the Philosophy of Sex and Love, to which Professor Singer has
kindly dedicated this new book of his.

During the years 1985 and 1986, while teaching at
St. John's University and the College of St. Benedict in
Minnesota, I eagerly read the recently published *Courtly
and Romantic* (1984), volume 2 of *The Nature of Love*, as
well as the second edition of the first volume, *Plato to
Luther*. (At the same time, living in a town populated
by only a few thousand people, I also, in the only coffee
shop around, finally made my way through Anders
Nygren's classic, *Agape and Eros*.) In 1987 I was already
devouring Professor Singer's volume 3, *The Modern
World*, when I was invited by a journal to review it for
its pages. Writing reviews is often a tedious chore, but
that assignment was a blessing and a joy.

In my own philosophical writing and lectures about
love and sex, whether focusing on Plato, Augustine,
Aquinas, Rousseau, Hume, Kant, Kierkegaard, Schopenhauer, Freud, or Sartre, I have found it useful—no,
essential—to return to the three volumes of *The Nature
of Love* over and over again, as well as to Professor
Singer's other books on love and sex. I have learned

much from him about the rich history of the philosophy of love, the fiction of love, the poetry of love, the music of love, and (to borrow Erich Fromm's phrase) the art of love. Reading his many books, I received an exquisite lesson about the meaning of the word *erudite*.

I have emphasized numerous times, in print and in conversations with curious students and colleagues: if you want to study the philosophy of love and sex, Professor Singer's trilogy should be at the top of your list. But having read his new book, which summarizes, explains, and elaborates various themes found in *The Nature of Love*, I realize that I wish this book had been available to me in my salad days, that I had read it before immersing myself in the entire trilogy. That is now what I will say to those potential students of the philosophy of love and sex who ask me where they should start. First this book, then *The Nature of Love*.

This book, as helpful as it would have been to me in graduate school, could not have been written before the trilogy. The specific reason is that it is a very personal book, a book in which Professor Singer reflects on both his life and his work, trying not only to understand more deeply the history of the idea of love but also to comprehend himself, to discover how he chose and handled his topics and why he arrived at his particular conclusions. The book, then, is as much an intellectual autobiography as it is an exploration of love and sex. And that adds to its fascination, giving us a glimpse of the thought processes of a scholar who has contributed so much to the humanities.

Alan Soble was Professor of Philosophy and University Research Professor at the University of New Orleans, 1986– 2006. After retiring from UNO, Soble moved to Philadelphia, where he now teaches philosophy at Drexel University and the Abington campus of Pennsylvania State University. The revised and expanded edition of his The Philosophy of Sex and Love: An Introduction *(Paragon House) was published in 2008.*

Prefatory Note

This book is a partial summing-up in several ways. It is partial because I have written it as an expression of my own preferential involvement with the philosophy of love. Here, as in my other writings on this topic, the philosophers I discuss reflect my personal sense of their importance as well as my individual estimation of what they affirm. While I try to be accurate in my assessments, as in my descriptions, I make no pretensions about definitive objectivity. Though at times I may seem to think of the history of the subject as leading to myself, I do not believe that I or anyone else can be its ultimate destination. I offer my writing only as the embodiment of what I have learned as a contemporary philosopher studying other authors in this field and trying to go a little further.

The present work is a summing-up twice over: first, in being a selective condensation of the ideational panorama that I draw upon and to which I have already devoted many published pages. Readers who may be plausibly deterred by the unpolemical character of this book might be comforted by the realization that more probing and more enlarged treatment of the issues occurs elsewhere in my writings. In places I mention their titles and some of their contents, but I refrain from duplicating what I have put into the original presentations.

The second form of partial summing-up pertains to the fact that I do not consider philosophy to be a subject that can have a culminating outcome or comprehensive solution to the varied questions it poses. No summation can therefore exclude ongoing and more fruitful addenda worth attaining. Reflecting on what I myself have done, I see only a string of approximations and reconsiderations without any reason to think that I am either closer to or more distant from an all-inclusive statement. I do not believe that love, or life for that matter, lends itself to either eventuality.

The text is intentionally more informal and less didactic than other books of mine that are related to it. I have wanted to offer a general perspective that readers without technical interest can readily digest and possibly enjoy. Toward that end I have avoided the use of footnotes, and references to remarks by other writers are normally reproduced in my own paraphrase rather than being quoted verbatim.

The material for this effort originated in a series of interviews I gave to a radio producer that sometimes turned into more of a monologue than a conversation. The casual setting of these discussions accounts for the colloquial character of what I have now put into words on a page. The unstructured format often elicited ideas that I could not previously bring to the surface. As a result, the book contains, within its occasionally amorphous framework, both new and old ideas of mine whose presentation here may be pleasing to some readers but unsatisfying to others. At the end of the manuscript, I recommend research that would involve cooperation between biological science and various humanistic approaches, yet I offer few intimations about the findings that might occur. This shortfall is particularly notable with respect to women's studies, in which very promising work is now beginning to emerge. I leave these areas to investigators who are more competent than I am, but also with a hope that my ruminations may somehow contribute to their empirical and likely impressive discoveries.

Finally and briefly, I want to place this book in the context of the decades of my personal cogitations that preceded it. As I say later on, I began my labors in the philosophy of love at a time when hardly any reputable philosophers in the Anglo-Saxon world considered that subject professional or even respectable. My working at it cut me loose from the mainstream of American philosophical analysis. Since I had nevertheless been trained as an analytical philosopher, I naturally (and naively) thought I would write a book that systematically examines in very precise detail the elements and the problematics that adhere to the ordinary use of the word *love*. As in almost everything I have undertaken intellectually, I was motivated by anxieties, confusions, unresolved ambivalences within myself as a human being and not merely as a thinker. Idle abstractions meant little to me then, or do so now, and I felt that I could overcome the dilemmas in my own affective life by a careful, albeit plodding, analysis of what matters to everyone.

In making the attempt, however, I found that the chapters I wrote were just dreary and unproductive. In my desperation, I thought that the history of ideas in philosophy and the arts might help me get restarted. What I unearthed was an immensity of speculation and aesthetic output that reached wholly beyond the parameters I had been trained to consider truly philosophical. My resultant trilogy, *The Nature of Love*, tried to make sense of this historical progression of thought and inspiration within a framework of distinctions that I myself imposed and that reflected whatever analytical talent I might still have.

By the time I finished the trilogy, I began to feel that my conceptualization was too sketchy, too narrow and incomplete. I realized that understanding love or its related conditions required an investigation into problems about meaningfulness in life as a whole and the human creation of value in general. After another nine years, that perception led to my second trilogy, *Meaning in Life*. All of that deals obliquely with the nature of love, and the second volume in it, subtitled *The Pursuit of Love*, is structured as a more or less nonhistorical treatment of questions about love that I was unable to confront before.

Even so, there still lingered problems about the relation between love and imagination, idealization, consummation, and the aesthetic. In the last few years I have grappled with them in books, notably *Feeling and Imagination: The Vibrant Flux of Our Existence* and *Explorations in Love and Sex*, that are organically derivative from my earlier studies on the nature of love. In their own way, something similar is true of my recent adventures in the philosophy and phenomenology of film as well as my current writings on the nature of creativity.

The summing-up that you are about to read scans that entire trajectory. It is an apologia pro mente sua, and an illustrated miniature of my life as a thinker or would-be philosopher.

I. S.

Philosophy of Love: A Partial Summing-Up

Is Romantic Love a Recent Idea?

When I started my trilogy *The Nature of Love*, many scholars believed that the concept of love as a romantic, sexual, or interpersonal phenomenon originated very recently—within the last two hundred years or so. I felt that this view did not correctly elucidate the history of ideas about these or any other kinds of love. In some respects it is true that the notion of romantic love as we know it today can be considered fairly novel. Nevertheless the received conception about it is far too incomplete. What we call romantic love belongs to an intellectual development that starts with the beginning of romanticism in the modern world. To that extent, the relevant idea is rightly designated (and capitalized) as "Romantic" love. It arose toward the end of the eighteenth century and began to flourish at the beginning of the nineteenth century. But even at the time, few people realized how traditional though also innovative this notion was: it stemmed from an evolutionary process in which theories about love had existed throughout two millennia.

To someone doing the kind of research I did, it was apparent that many elements of nineteenth-century Romantic love derived from sources in ancient Greek philosophy and literature, in Hellenistic fables, in the burgeoning of Christianity, in the reaction against Christianity during the Renaissance, and then in a diversity of seventeenth- and early-eighteenth-century modes of thought. You can't really separate this continuum into two periods, the first of which was prior to any ideas about Romantic love and the other consisting in the thinking of the last two hundred years with its great focus on it. The claim that Romantic love is an *invention* of the latter period is therefore of limited value, and, on the face of it, mistaken.

Yet there was clearly something important and very special that did happen in this modern movement, and we are still living with its ongoing development. It's passed through several phases, some of which I have spent hundreds of pages writing about. The second volume of *The Nature of Love*, for instance, is subtitled

Courtly and Romantic. When I get to Romantic love in the nineteenth century, I distinguish between a type of optimistic romanticism, what I call benign romanticism, and a totally different kind, very prominent about 1850, that I label Romantic pessimism. Earlier there had been foreshadowings of both forms of ideology in the plays of Shakespeare. In various ways he spoke as a critic of what we nowadays call "courtly love," which blossomed in the Middle Ages and for almost five hundred years. As against courtly love, Shakespeare articulated concepts that ultimately turned into nineteenth-century Romantic views about love, both the benign and the pessimistic. Shakespeare was an important contributor to their formulation.

While writing this second volume of my trilogy—a long book, over five hundred pages in length—I didn't calculate in advance where to put Shakespeare. But as it turned out, and as I discovered when the chapters were finished, he ended up right in the middle. In fact Shakespeare is a pivotal figure. Being a thinker whose mentality issues out of courtly love and against courtly love, he anticipates, but does not fully announce, what will later become Romantic attitudes toward medieval philosophy of love. As in many other ways, Shakespeare is a very rare type of genius, one whose artistic creativity became a primal force in Western

intellectual history. Though Romantics in the nineteenth century often treated him like one of themselves,
he is not a full-fledged adherent to romanticism.
Without being a Romantic philosopher or theorist, he
is nevertheless a precursor of those who were.

As illustration, take the play *Much Ado About
Nothing,* which Kenneth Branagh made into a popular
movie. It is structured in terms of two kinds of love.
One is the relationship between Claudio and Hero, the
young man and woman who have a courtly
relationship based on very little understanding of
themselves or of each other, and not including much
more than their awareness that they have both fallen in
love. Though they strongly *feel* they love each other,
Shakespeare demolishes the authenticity of their attachment. He shows how Claudio falsely accuses Hero of
infidelity, while he himself isn't faithful since, instead
of handling whatever problems he may have with this
woman, he immediately condemns and humiliates her.
Their bond therefore comes out as emotionally suspect.
The other relation is the bellicose but ultimately loving
tie between Benedick and Beatrice. They have a natural
attunement that shows itself in ways that are typically
Romantic. Romanticism frequently presupposes a basic
hostility between male and female. It takes this to be a
deeply innate tendency resulting from the fact that,

being differently programmed, the sexes do not see the world in the same manner. As a consequence, each is natively suspicious of the opposite gender, and in a state of constant warfare with it.

There's support for that view in work that recent biologists have done, for instance, with herring gulls in the mating season when the female arrives on an isolated island by herself. She maps out her terrain and waits for the males to come. But as soon as one of them enters her property, she attacks him. Only after a period of what scientists call "equilibration" do they work out some mutual understanding, and she realizes that he is what she has been wanting for reproductive purposes. She then lets him onto her terrain, and they become a romantic couple. Well, the same kind of thing happens to human beings within the Romantic frame of thought, and it's what happens to Beatrice and Benedick. They are born enemies, ridiculing each other at first, but then, because of a quirk in the plot that Shakespeare artificially but deftly arranges, they overcome their initial belligerence.

Having done that, the two who are now one are able to help their friends—the courtly lovers who can't make things work out by themselves—and in helping them, their own bond becomes stronger. Beatrice and Benedick act together in a companionate and fully satisfying alliance. Even though they joke about their mutual animosity, they experience a consummate love. Both pairs get married, but we surmise that Beatrice and Benedick are much more likely to succeed in marriage than the other couple. Only the embattled ones understand each other, and, having survived their initial animosity, they are capable of attaining wholesome unification. For them the inherent disdain among people of different genders has been successfully overcome.

Despite the bumps and quarrels and all the tribulations that occur in the marital state, we feel that Beatrice and Benedick may really live happily ever after. We can't be sure what it will be like for Hero and her young man—the other pair. That confrontation between courtly and Romantic is presented in the works of Shakespeare better perhaps than in almost anyone else's. And most of the elements in his thinking, processed over an expanse of three hundred years, enter into the residue of Romantic love that still exists today. The common belief that true love as conceived in the nineteenth century was all sweetness and light is a fallacy.

Even in the benign phase there was recognition of the difficulty in obtaining authentic oneness, apart from any outside interference from social expectations about marriage and courtship and, of course, from parental control. It was understood that males and females were significantly unlike each other, and even incompatible in many ways. But there remained the hope, the dream, that those difficulties could be surmounted. This typically Romantic view is what Shakespeare had portrayed. It is why I think of him as a great pivotal figure. All the same, he is only one among many others who constructed ideas about the human search for love that have been developing in the last two thousand years and more.

Plato

As the beginning of my historical approach, I start with Plato. I have always felt that he is the greatest philosopher who ever lived. And he is the father of philosophy, if you don't count Socrates, who never wrote anything. Plato is certainly the beginning of the great exploration in the philosophy of love that occurred in the Western world. But Plato was very complex as a philosopher. For instance, consider the androgynous couples described in *The Symposium*, one of his middle-period dialogues. The person in that work who recites the relevant myth is not Plato himself, but Aristophanes. Moreover, *The Symposium* is just one of various works that Plato wrote at the time, some of which are very different from it.

The crucial thing about the hermaphroditic creatures in Aristophanes' fable, as reported by Plato, is there being three types after the gods split them. Originally only a single kind existed, but when the gods divided each of the hermaphrodites into two halves (because they were getting overly arrogant) there resulted three modes of reunification for which they strove. One was a bonding of males and females looking for each other. In addition, there was the attachment of two females, making a lesbian couple, and also the craving for oneness between two males. In other words, you already have implied in Plato the questioning about same-sex as distinct from opposite-sex affiliations that recurs in all the present controversy about marriage in America and elsewhere.

Aristophanes says that, among these three arrangements, the best combination is the one of two males. Athens was a male-dominated society, and the little cluster that Plato belonged to at that time was largely homosexual—a gay nucleus within the Athenian and Greek community. Not all Greek states were as tolerant of homosexuality as Athens was, and it was surely not universal in Athenian society either. So people who have thought that everyone in Athens was gay are not right at all. But Plato in his youth probably did belong to a homoerotic group of one sort or another. Though some members may only have been friends or mentors, many must have had overtly sexual relations.

Even so, the later Plato takes a very different stand. Once you come to *The Laws,* which is an important book that Plato wrote toward the end of his life, when he was almost eighty, you find that he attacks homosexuality. He says that the only kind of family that the state should encourage is a biological unit in which there is a marriage between "one man and one woman." He can even be cited in support of the constitutional amendment about the nature of marriage that some people in the United States are trying to enact. Consequently, Plato's final ideas were quite unlike anything he had said in *The Symposium, Phaedrus,* and other dialogues. Also, in *The Republic*, which is perhaps the greatest book ever written in Western philosophy—certainly one of the few greatest books—Plato talks about sex and love in a manner that goes beyond his remarks in *The Symposium* and *Phaedrus*, and even in *The Laws.* In *The Republic*, he asserts that we are all designed to search for the Good. And when we are in love, the body is used in that endeavor as an agency of instinctual, reproductive forces. These are what Freud

would call libidinal urges toward heterosexual love-
making, coital sex. That is fine and natural, according
to Plato, but not the ultimate goal of humanity. The
point is to get beyond bodily imperatives in order to
pursue the Good, as the only means through which
people can fulfill their spiritual being and find what is
of value and truly beautiful in life.

How do you make that transition from sex-driven
impulses as a young person to having other, more
elevated, interests? By throwing yourself into meri-
torious endeavors, Plato claims—into art and the
appreciation of the aesthetic, into the formation of a
desirable society, into the quest for scientific truths, and
into other cognitive means of revealing an ultimate
reality that is not reducible simply to sex. The proper
response to sexual instinct itself, Plato argues, is
promiscuity. Have as much sex as you want, he says, as
early as you want with anybody you choose, regardless
of who it is and whatever the gender of that other
person may be. You will discover that the particular
objects of sexual activity are all alike. Having
fully sampled sex, he predicts, you will have then
outgrown it.

My older brother, when he was young, hated the
idea that he loved hamburgers. He cured himself by
gorging on them once, and the appetite disappeared.

He never wanted to eat hamburgers in later life to the extent that he did before, because he had made himself sick on them. That was Plato's advice about sex—that you gorge yourself, at an early age, as much as society allows. The situation is very much like South Sea Island attitudes that the anthropologist Bronislaw Malinowski encountered at the beginning of the twentieth century. He observed that the young could do whatever they wished, and the parents didn't care. It was only sex. It was of no great significance. Plato's idea is that once you have cleansed yourself of the fanatical drive caused by those hormonal instincts that are surging during adolescence to prepare you for reproductive necessities of the species—once you have had all that you can stand of that, you won't be driven by sexual need, and, in any event, it won't be a prime motivation for you.

Instead you might start thinking about love, and even fall in love with some individual. But there too, Plato asserts, you may eventually get beyond personal attachment—interpersonal romantic love—and this liberation will initiate the course of education that can enable you to perceive the Good, which is fundamental in the universe and which is what in Christianity becomes the principal attribute of God. The "Good" is the highest form of being in Christianity: by his very nature as divinity, God is perfectly good, perfectly beautiful, and the supremely perfect origin of reality. That whole part of Christianity comes directly or indirectly out of Platonism.

But see how this implicates a kind of love that differs vastly from what arises in primordial nature. You might end up with spiritual love, religious love, the love of God, however you interpret these words, and that will be far from where you started biologically. In between there might be the love of the truth that the philosopher has, the love of factual and theoretical investigation that scientists have, the love of one's people, one's country, one's nation, such that you devote yourself to making laws that are fair and equitable for everyone in the state. Likewise there may be the love that a warrior has, showing his devotion to his homeland by fighting and possibly dying for it. All of that takes you beyond sex, while also remaining part of the same continuum since sex too has to be understood as a product of our search for the Good and Beautiful as the basis for any love a human being can attain.

This Platonic doctrine is, I believe, the most fertile and powerful single body of thought about love that anyone has ever created throughout Western civilization. Out of it came not only Christianity but also the reaction against Christianity, together with all sorts of

Neoplatonic as well as anti-Platonic views introduced by philosophers like Aristotle, who approached these ideas as a pupil of Plato but dealt with them differently. Platonism is a momentous stage in the mind of man that every educated person should be schooled in. It is worth studying endlessly.

Beyond Idealism

Whether or not I am right in this opinion, we still have to recognize that history—the history of ideas in this case—doesn't march in a linear fashion. Ideational changes are like the fluctuations in the stock market. They go in one direction and then there is a reaction against them. The greatness of Hegel consisted in his sensitivity to this dialectic among ideas. In fact he used it as a mode of understanding all of reality. I don't agree with him on that, any more than I agree with Plato, but I do think that the notion of a fluctuating dialectic helps us comprehend how, in the passage of time, you get schools of thought among the anti-Platonists that delineate love in alternate ways while also being responsive to what Plato and the platonistic philosophers said.

It is in this context that one should see the work of David Hume. He did not believe in metaphysics of the type that Plato proferred. Nor was he a Romantic. He was a pre-Romantic empiricist. A modern-day existentialist, or pragmatistic humanist and pluralist, which I am, also approaches things from an empirical point of view that doesn't fit the Platonic mold and yet, particularly in my case, can appreciate the seductiveness in that kind of thought. For Hume and his successors, the lowest rung in the ladder of Plato's vision, the one that focuses on the world of experience and materiality that everyone inhabits, is quite sufficient for its own philosophical comprehension. Instead of having to think about the Platonic trajectory, which is a vertical concept about ascending to transcendental heights above and beyond what is natural, we prefer more horizontal perspectives. They in turn enable us to understand love in terms of diversities within nature itself.

I feel very strongly about this, because I think that humans, and their fundamental types of relations—such as love—are ineluctibly plural. I am convinced that studying different features of our being at an empirical level close to the facticity of nature is probably the best we can hope for. I'm not a Platonist because Plato assumes that there is one answer to the universe, that he knows what it must be, and that it involves the idealistic analysis he advocates. In my derivation from thinkers like Hume and John Stuart Mill and John Dewey, and modern empiricism in general, I believe that instead of looking for one answer, especially of the transcendental type that Plato seeks, we should ask questions about reality and what is valuable in it as persons who recognize the variegated character of their involvement in nature.

My work as a whole is of that sort. Someone asked Ludwig Wittgenstein, the great twentieth-century philosopher, what he did for a living, and he replied, "I'm a maker of analogies." It is actually true to what he did do; he showed a good deal of insight into his own talent. In the same vein, I would say that I'm a maker of distinctions. And the more distinctions I make, the more varied are the aspects in which I am able to think about the nature of love. I don't promote any a prioristic or overarching theory. I'm very suspicious of that. I don't think that large-scale terms like love, happiness, meaning of life, meaning in life, sex, beauty, and such, are able to have any one definition. These phenomena are so enormous within our human nature—and the same is true of what we even mean by human nature—that we cannot justifiably constrict them within a single, fixed and all-embracing, defini-tion of the kind that Plato sought. The most we can do is to clarify them with ever-finer analysis or dissection, and to engage in further explorations through new though possibly sequential distinctions. Only then can we correlate and combine our ideas by means of the creative speculations that will issue forth without there being any one and only principle that draws everything into itself. There will always be realities of feeling and experience that do not fit.

Concepts of Transcendence and Merging

Though Plato had the greatest cumulative effect of all Western philosophers, his mode of philosophizing was rejected by Nietzsche at the end of the nineteenth century in a fashion that seems to me very telling. Repudiating the Platonic kind of thought, Nietzsche also reviles Socrates for being what he calls the "archetype of the intellectual man." He attacks him in *The Birth of Tragedy Out of Music*. Nietzsche thought that Greek tragedy deteriorated once the intellectual man, represented by Socrates, dominated the culture. I feel that's mistaken, and I have criticized Nietzsche accordingly in my book *Feeling and Imagination*. But I think that his rejection of Plato is inspiring. He didn't adequately understand the importance of Socrates' work, while I myself am happy to think that I am basically a Socratic philosopher.

Socrates argued that we all know what reality is. We all know concretely what such deep concepts mean, though we are confused in our thoughts. The job of a philosopher is therefore to help us make our ideas clear. That's what I also try to do. But in the process we have to give up the notion that there can be a conclusive answer to "the human problem." Something along those lines may exist in mathematics—if you don't give the right answer, you don't get the correct sum for 2 plus 2 equals—but life is not a mathematical problem. And, consequently, one should not look for a unitary solution to the nature of love or expect to find, for example, that the modern age is or is not out of touch with the great realm of being that Plato and medieval Christianity claimed to discern. Instead of asserting anything like that, we need to see and appreciate what has been happening in the world of human *searching* for one or another solution. Only as we pinpoint the contents of this pursuit can we have viable ideas about some particular facet of our reality—which is to say, our nature as ever-questing beings.

In that attempt, I examine two major themes in Plato's philosophy that were to have a large effect upon all later thinking: the notions of transcendence and of merging. I am an opponent of both. I don't believe that human love can be explained in terms of a transcendence into a higher reality. We are products of the manifold forces that operate on this planet. Love is limited to that, and it cannot be explained by reference to a metaphysical domain beyond our earthly condition. Neither do I agree with the idea that merging of any kind is what we are really interested in when we talk about love. In general, I am an enemy of the common belief in merging. It is not true about human capacity, and in fact it is a very dangerous idea.

This is not to say that merging is impossible. It occurs in salt every day—in the conjunction of sodium and chloride. And it happens when rivulets come together and make a stream. In each case, once the interpenetration has taken place, you can't tell the elements apart. They've merged. We often use that word, and in those circumstances it's a perfectly normal mode of speaking. Also there is a musical occurrence in which the notes merge and make a new and interesting combination. If you strike a chord on the piano, you cause a merging in the sound. My argument is that this is not true to what it is to be a person, to be a living creature like us. We, as human beings, and in our attempt to love others, do not exist as rivulets, but rather as different individuals. In our personhood we do not merge; we cannot merge. The most that can happen is that because you think you're merging, you end up falsifying ingredients in the reality of your relationship.

As a result of their *desire* to merge—and it's a feeling that some people find very attractive—men and women distort themselves in one respect or another. This alone justifies the doubt that love can ever be an actual merging. There is a kind of romanticism that predicates a basic hunger in everyone for some such fusion. Without denying the frequency of this aspiration, I see little reason to think that it is characteristic of all forms of romantic attachment, and I'm sure that it is not fulfilled in any actual instances of love. In the history of philosophy one can find more plausible descriptions. They refer to other forms of relationships, usually Aristotelian and not Platonic. They rely upon concepts of people who interpenetrate; who have a bond that is interpersonal; who may be interdependent upon each other's personality; who are companionate; who share their separate selves; who each discover someone who is significantly different and with whom one neither submits nor blindly subjects oneself to whatever the other is and wants.

In those circumstances, both persons recognize that they are indefeasibly not the same. But out of this recognition of diversity, and in the mutual acceptance of it, can come a sense of oneness. Something similar applies to concepts like "the United States" or "the United Nations." Those were great ideas that arose at the end of the eighteenth century and along the lines I am describing. It isn't that everybody in every state and every nation becomes identical because they have all fused together in accordance with some ideal pattern of merging. But rather there is an acknowledgment of real disparity, depending on the region, the history, and the individual type of governance to which human beings revert while also being united in crucial ways. That seems to me to be what love is like most definitively. In those countries in which everyone is forced into a single mold, totalitarian countries in particular, the nation tries to live up to an icon of conformity that is comparable to treating love as merging. I consider those totalitarian nations inferior, and the congruent affective philosophies erroneous about the nature of love.

The notion of merging was especially prominent at the beginning of the nineteenth century. When people speak of romantic love being a recent occurrence, they do so because merging took on greatest importance at that time. The Romantic theorists treated merging as central to the conception of love they had in mind. The doctrine also issues from other views in the history of ideas. Medieval Christianity was perennially divided by a controversy about merging. Some illustrious thinkers were burned at the stake because they thought that men or women could merge with God. In Islam, too, there was a great philosopher who was executed because he said, "I am God." What he meant wasn't that he was part of the personhood of a supernatural being. He meant that he had merged with God in the sense of total unity, at oneness, with him. Taken literally, that idea was heretical for Islam as it was for Christianity. It might also have been troublesome in Judaism except that the relevant conception is very remote from the Jewish idea of loving God as a unique and separate being. In Catholicism, with its platonistic origins, the notion posed a pervasive puzzlement.

In Catholic theology, you find the assertion that God is *in* the world. Scholars and fathers of the church disagreed about how this could be the case. Some said that God is in the world because he is present throughout nature. But then that sounds like pantheism—as if God is the same as nature, inseparable from it. Christianity did not tolerate an approach of that sort, since it runs counter to the basic tenet that God has a different and more sublime being. God was inherently beyond nature, and nature itself was impure and imperfect—possibly evil. The body was to be contrasted with the soul, and therefore God couldn't be literally in the material world. He belonged to a spiritual realm toward which we mortals could only aspire. If we were lucky enough to have divine grace, or perfected ourselves through good works, we might nevertheless be admitted to the supernatural domain. That was all the ruling dogma in Christianity allowed. At the same time, many people did think that God was somehow also in us and in the world as a whole. This, however, created the massive problem for ecclesiastical authorities that centers around the question of merging. As against this notion, the more moderate concept of "wedding" was often invoked.

Throughout the Middle Ages there existed references to man wedding God—being wedded to God. The human soul was the bride, and God was the bridegroom. This theme recurs in a good deal of medieval religious poetry. The two beings were conjoined not in the sense that they merge but rather because they get wedded or even welded together. They communicate and ultimately interpenetrate without losing their individual substance. The finite human being could thus achieve a kind of oneness that saturates the soul with the goodness of God while he or she still remained separate from the deity. That was common parlance in the Middle Ages, and it is in this vein that I also talk about wedding. It is intelligible as opposed to merging.

If you look at the poetry of St. Teresa, you'll see that a lot of it sounds as if she may well have believed in merging, or at least was entertaining it as a possibility. But that was not the orthodox view, and even today it is not accepted at face value by the Catholic Church. It is normally taken as a form of idolatry akin to loving another human being with the kind of religious love that only God merits.

Nowadays the love between men and women, and men or women, is sometimes treated as if it alone were religious love. This attitude, which many Romantics in the nineteenth century openly defended, is a disposition that the church always feared: if people had quasi-religious love of each other, they would be enacting a disservice to God and not living up to his commandment about being loved uniquely. Thou shalt love thy God with all thy heart, with all thy might, and with all thy soul. But you can't do that if you are going to love your girlfriend or your boyfriend that way. Consequently, the very suggestion was heresy in the Middle Ages. Out of that conflict between the orthodox view and the heretical attachment to another person, particularly if you think you are merging with this person and having the feelings the church said mortals should have toward God, there arose the kind of medieval and courtly myth that is present in the legend of Tristan and Iseult. Because of the love potion, the two people love each other with a total giving of themselves and with explicit belief in the goodness of merging with one another. That myth is especially evident to us in Wagner's opera, which was written in the Romantic period but was preceded by hundreds of related versions of the legend in earlier centuries.

The church was concerned that its mission would be impaired by any human love that mimicked the devotion you should have for the deity. The love potion could only be an evil that leads to a tragic ending. And, indeed, in many nations, the love of God may have become in our age less pervasive than the search for love of another man or woman. Statistics about how many people go to church indicate that in the United States a large number do, in Spain very few, and in France and other European countries hardly any. It is difficult to know what is happening among the young, and whether they are emancipating themselves from the dominance of the traditional faith by trying to find in another human being something equivalent to the love of God. But disillusionment about supernatural beliefs has surely increased. Moreover, those who exist in the modern world are aware of how imperfect any interpersonal arrangements must be under actual conditions, and therefore how hard it is to live up to the older ideals of love. And, even if you follow established mandates, it can all be a big mistake, since you may not get what you really want. You undergo anxiety and misery, individuals as well as institutional teachings delude you, and you run the risk of being betrayed by an idealistic ideology that mattered to you.

In relation to merging, Nietzsche states in one place: "If there are Gods, how is it possible that I'm not one of them?" As facetious and humorous as he was trying to be, Nietzsche touches a profound explanation of the search for merging. If you believe in God as perfection, you as a human being will not only snuggle up to him in the hope of getting his protection, Nietzsche suggests, you will also want to *be* what he is. Sartre develops this very far in *Being and Nothingness*. Man is a futility, he says, because man wants to be God, and there is no God. But what lurks beneath this conception is *why* someone would want to be God, to merge with God. It's because one has the image of a perfect being. There may conceivably be such a being, and the human imagination that goes into thinking about this possibility is itself a very high achievement that I do not wish to demean in any way. The ideal entity is something you would want to merge with just as you would want to be perfect on your own. A man or woman might, in principle, acquire this perfection simply by merging with it.

That's one understanding of the origin of the quest for merging. Another is the fact that we all begin with a kind of merging. It happens when the sperm and the egg collide. They don't just shake hands and say, "Let's live together and survive however well we can," as in the ending of *Candide,* the musical by Leonard Bernstein: "We're neither pure nor wise nor good. / We'll do the best we know. / We'll build our house and chop our wood / and make our garden grow."

That may be the highest goal, the highest love that Candide can hope for after all the calamities that he and Cunégonde have been through. Even so, the advent of human love cannot occur by biological means alone. In the act of reproduction, the sperm throws itself into the egg, and the zygote is made in a flash of merging. It's a chemical event just like salt being made out of its components. But the reproductive occurrence is only a prelude to the human story. One reason that I believe in the morality of abortion is because those who attack it say, "Oh, you're killing a person." Well, the zygote isn't a person. And once personhood comes into the individual development of men and women, we've moved beyond the possibility of merging. It was once a part of us, just as the food we've eaten all our lives is a part of us. But, as persons, we become something more, and no longer capable of merging in the way that cells or molecular elements do.

A hope of this latter sort may underlie the reasoning of people who say or feel: If only I could return to some kind of primordial, biologically programmed state, my amatory problems would all disappear. It's like people wanting to return to the womb, which is a notion of Freud's—his belief that all men want to do so. I wonder why he didn't say the same about women. They also came out of a womb. In any event, these notions about merging are sports of the imagination that can be very intriguing, and the aesthetics of their formulation throughout the history of ideas has always fascinated me. So I am not suggesting that one shouldn't even think about merging. The *thought* of it is an integral feature of our mentality as creative beings, inasmuch as it issues from speculation that makes us inventive and imaginative. But the concept itself is not true to our reality, what we are as human beings. The nature of love must therefore be elucidated in other, less fanciful, ways.

Courtly Love and Its Successors

Returning to ancient Greek philosophy, we should always remember that it issues from a society and culture that was very narrowly specified. It's not only that the ideas focused upon people who were upper-class, and not only because they were males, but also because they were members of an elitist state in which women were subjugated. There were also 400,000 slaves in Athens, and they too had no voice. We have no means of knowing what their ideas of love were. Daily life was very remote from the democratic ideals that have emanated out of it indirectly, and that most Americans espouse. The Greek city-states were not only sexist and class-ridden but thoroughly autocratic as well. I think they were probably a very peculiar phenomenon in human existence. It just happens that there were many geniuses among those people, or at least many outstanding men among them, from whom we can learn a great deal. But as far as their thinking about love is concerned, it reflected an outlook that was alien to the views we have nowadays. I would put it into its historical place instead of using it as a model.

With the advent of courtly love in the Middle Ages, things began to change. But before that there was the emergence of Christianity out of Judaism and Greek thought. When I wrote my love trilogy, the chapter that I liked most of all at the time was the one on agapē, the Christian idea of God's bestowal of his love. That is a momentous concept in world history. My own thinking about bestowal initially resulted from reading Bishop Nygren's book *Agape and Eros*. It seemed to me that his conception of agapē was misguided inasmuch as it maintains both that love originates from God and that it originates *only* from God. I have always considered love a projection of what people do, or are trying to do all the time, and that only if we accept the reality of this kind of projection can we construct an adequate theory of human love. In other words, I wanted to stand the Christian notion on its head, or (if I'm right) on its feet. But while I don't agree with the way it was presented by Nygren, and is still affirmed by Christians, I see the conception of agapē as a fertile occurrence in human-kind's ability to understand what love may be.

Courtly love has a role to play because it was an effort to humanize Christian thought in the Middle Ages. The attempt is very meaningful to me. It is based on a love of nature, not merely as God's product but as in itself worthy of love. There were Christian courtly thinkers and there were non-Christian courtly thinkers. Much of the difference between them depends on how the relationship between God and nature is interpreted.

But the idea of humanizing love—the belief that love is something that one can have not only in relation to God, but also and magnificently with another human being, particularly a person of the opposite sex—that belief about what is valuable in life is a development beyond the thinking that preceded it. It's not the case, as some writers have said (Denis de Rougemont, for instance), that the idea of romantic love was *created* in the Middle Ages. In the Hellenistic period, there were descriptions of heterosexual romantic love that were comparable. The point about courtly love is that it occurs after the growth and widespread dominance of Christian ideology. And so it's a mechanism for relating to another person with the same kind of attachment that the church ordained in the love of God. This alone was a major achievement, which went on for several hundred years, from about the end of the twelfth century or beginning of the thirteenth to the time of Shakespeare in the sixteenth and seventeenth century—with all sorts of ups and downs and complex fluctuations.

Throughout this period, love between human beings was given ever greater social and political importance that reflected what was happening in the history of ideas. As a general rule, creative minds don't operate in a vacuum; they come out of living soil and then contribute to it willy-nilly, depending on what exactly has gone before and what is happening and fruitful in the present. You could have a prodigy who is alienated from his origins, but he probably won't be remembered; he won't have any effect. But the promoters of courtly love were very much in touch with their environment, and so the outlook was able to exist and to flourish for those several hundred years. It doesn't much remain in the modern world.

At the same time, courtly love contributed directly, and in its own fashion, to the democratization of love with which we are now familiar. It was, for the Middle Ages, democratization in a very narrow sense. While the Greeks thought of the elite, the philosophers, the philosopher-kings, as people who were able to love—and the only ones who were—the courtly period tended to include other human beings as well. Of course, they weren't just ordinary folk. They were the feudal lords and ladies, the aristocrats in the Middle Ages, and not participants in anything similar to the intellectual life of fourth-century BC Athens. This shift was, however, a move in the direction that eventually culminated in the idea that almost anyone could love, and do it well. It was part of the democratization that has happened in Western history in many aspects of life and over several centuries.

As I previously remarked, we do not know what
was happening affectively at the lower levels of medieval society. Occasionally a woman of higher rank had
a lover who was socially inferior—possibly a poet who
celebrated her beauty and charm. But I wouldn't want
to define courtly love in only those terms. The period
in history lasted a long time and spread across Europe
and the Near East. The men, the rulers, the princes,
the warriors went off to conquer other countries. They
were away on the crusades, while their wives remained
at home with the job of running the state. Women like
Eleanor of Aquitaine and some others became very
powerful within their own little principality or kingdom.
And certainly that gave them greater allure that could
be extolled by the itinerant poets who wrote verses for
the ruling female, whom they also claimed to love.

As a further complication, there were divergent
kinds of courtly love. It was not the same in the north
as in the south. In Southern France the poets were
expected not to be adulterous with their queen or
princess. One doesn't know what the truth was, but the
facade maintained that they were merely entertainers
writing love poetry for and about the monarch. Those
were the troubadours. The concept relevant to them
is called "fin' amors," which means pure love. In
the north, among the trouvères, there was another

tradition, in which love that was adulterous or carnal and fully sexual had its place as well.

Consequently, there were very different perceptions of what the nature of the "courtliness" was. There isn't any *single* notion of courtly love. I always try to make distinctions in order to see the variability in all of these gross and simpleminded ideas that find their way into schoolbooks. The reality is usually much more complicated. Particularly in terms of love, all the different streams and rivulets intertwine at every moment, regardless of any preconceived definition.

In my chapters on courtly love in volume 2 of the trilogy, I analyze several respects in which it differed from what preceded it. There are things one can say about courtly love itself that equally pertain to its different varieties. One was its tendency to dignify human relations between a man and a woman to a degree that had not existed when marriage was just an institutional device to bring families together for political or financial purposes, or to live up to the church's sanctified method of regulating reproduction. In courtly love, it is the ardent connecting of the right man and woman that ennobles them both and puts each in a superior condition. This could happen apart from wedlock, but married people were not necessarily excluded from having courtly love for each other. You didn't have to be adulterous or unmarried—as de Rougemont and C. S. Lewis claim—in order for there to be this kind of love. You could have both courtly love and monogamous marriage. In principle they were separable but also capable of coexisting in one way or another.

Though the women were sometimes dominant, or more knowledgeable about what a lover should be, the medieval romances often tell another type of story. The fourteenth-century tale of Aucassin and Nicolette is a good example. In it, Aucassin is a young boy, an aristocrat, who falls in love with a slave girl named Nicolette whom his father owns. He shocks his parents when he says he wants to marry her. They retort, "What do you mean, marry? You can do anything you want with her, but you have to marry someone who belongs to your social class." Aucassin can't take that, and so he runs away with the girl and they cohabit. They live together like married people and have exploits that cement their relationship. They are separated when a band of Muslims captures them. Aucassin doesn't see Nicolette for a long time, during which he has many adventures on his own. Eventually he is taken prisoner by a Muslim prince, whose wife turns out to be Nicolette. She recognizes Aucassin and still loves him. They cooperate and finally contrive to get free of the man with whom she has been living. The couple go back to Burgundy, where it all began. Aucassin's parents have died, and he becomes the ruler. He inherits the wealth and position that are rightly his, and he and Nicolette live happily ever after.

That is a typical medieval romance, and in many details it fits the pattern of courtly love. It is particularly interesting because the most heroic figure, or rather one of the two heroes, is a woman, and a slave girl! You don't find an exact equivalent in ancient Greek writings. There are inklings of it in Hellenistic fables, but the medieval depiction is part of a different and much larger perspective that was spreading throughout Europe in the Middle Ages and eventually fed into Western romanticism.

Before this occurred, there were intervening movements within seventeenth-century Puritanism and Rationalism, both of which reevaluate what would count as romantic love (with a little "r"). They derive only partly from ideas that were characteristic of the courtly period. Though the Puritans were not what we call "puritanical," they wanted to have a sensible approach to human sexuality and emotion within a religious framework that was coherent with their Protestant beliefs. These in turn showed the influence of Luther, whose views were inimical to the basic humanism of courtly love. In the case of the Rationalists, many of them questioned the goodness of love to begin with. They held that people should devote themselves to making their thoughts clearer and more cogent, instead of giving themselves to emotional excitement that inevitably undermines the power of reason.

Shakespeare comes on the scene as someone post-Luther who is aware of a good many of these countercurrents and who organizes them in terms of his splendidly dramatic dialectic on the stage. After Shakespeare there are theorists who carry further his kind of approach, though they don't envisage him as a philosophical source. The prevailing progression moves away from courtliness while also allowing a remnant of it to emerge in a version that is more suitable to later European society. In the nineteenth century, and under the influence of the French Revolution, whose ideas of equality, fraternity, and liberty encouraged people to love whomever they wished without parental interference, romanticism came into being. It brought together varied strands of thought and tried to construct an ideology by which individuals, particularly young men and women, would be able to attain an affective state of being that might variably amalgamate the previous views in the history of ideas that we have been discussing.

In this context, the role of women greatly changed. Female egalitarianism that is so important nowadays is a realization of what many Romantics believed in at the beginning of the nineteenth century. After the French Revolution, women were emancipated in some of the ways men were. Throughout the eighteenth century in Europe, there had been a great deal of freedom of sexual behavior, usually on the part of the men, though the women also could decide whom they wanted. They had access to greater sexual liberty than there had been for them when the church was all-powerful. In the nineteenth century, women strove for complete freedom. The Empress Josephine, and various prominent women, saw no reason why they couldn't have lovers just as their menfolk did. In more recent history, women have asserted themselves as having other capacities for which they don't need romantic love in order to achieve their personal goals, or at least not as much as was previously thought. And if they did experience romantic love, they would do so as free and autonomous agents rather then as persons who have to obtain their liberation *by means of* their love.

Yet that too is a fulfillment of the original conception of Romantic love. It was to happen through the egality that women are starting to have only now. In the current world women have shown that in most of the areas in which men excel, women can do so equally, and often better. As a result, women don't have to submit to romantic love as a means of satisfying some dominant male. What results, at least in principle, is thus a greater ability to indulge in romantic love for women who so desire, together with a greater freedom from the necessity to love in order to demonstrate one's inherent value. Both patterns of romanticism are therefore accentuated. Women can freely have romantic love as much as men can, but women can also do without it if they choose since they don't have to justify their existence in that manner or yield at all to the male's craving to have female lovers whenever he wants. I think we are going through a very exciting era, the two hundred years since the Romantic revolution having shattered affective and interpersonal molds that prevailed throughout the world. I don't despair of the future, except perhaps in having to live through the creation of it!

Varieties of Romantic Love

Jean-Jacques Rousseau is an important figure in relation to one kind of Romantic love, what I call Romantic puritanism. Though Rousseau was largely puritanical, he promoted the glorification of feelings and a gamut of vaguely sentimental ideas about love. That approach typifies a major segment of romanticism. It maintains that you can be a true lover even if you never have sex with anybody, or if you never marry your beloved, just by living in a hazy dream of oneness that typifies an early stage of individual maturation. Many adolescents or prepubescent boys and girls have such experience, and then most of them get over it. In Rousseau's type of romanticism, the benign sentiments suffice to make your life meaningful. And if they are puristically puritanical, they might not lead to anything else. Rousseau was a great prophet for this attitude, while living differently himself, since his whole life was not given over to the mere expression of sentiment. But there were other variations of romanticism as well.

Here again we encounter the value of pluralism that alerts you to expect diversity, while also keeping your eye on some unique historical circumstances in which the diversity occurs. If you compare Rousseau with Stendhal, as I do in a couple of chapters, you find two distinct types of romanticism. Though love, as Stendhal realistically portrays it in his novels, is always deceptive, he also affirms that human happiness cannot occur unless one succumbs to the illusions it creates. And there are other writers in this period who say something similar but whose ideas I didn't go into as thoroughly as I would have liked. One of them is Alfred de Musset—the poet and playwright—who in the middle of the nineteenth century transitioned from benign romanticism to Romantic pessimism, combining both in his literary productions. Though being very sophisticated about the disasters that are latent in Romantic love, he was also aware of how powerful and exhilarating it can be. He tries to work out some form of harmonization between these alternatives, but he usually ends by giving up in despair.

In its totality, Musset's approach differs from either Rousseau's or Stendhal's. In the twentieth century it leads into the negativism of Proust—who is nonetheless sensitive to the aesthetic wonderment of Romantic love, emanating as it does from an extraordinarily fertile use of the imagination. All the same, Proust thinks that, since it is based on an illusion, Romantic love is always doomed. The only love he truly accepts or appreciates, and I think the only one he really understands, is the love of art. He has a kind of Romantic view of art. Despite this limitation, Proust is probably the greatest philosophical novelist who ever lived, mainly because he is so perceptive about the contrasting values in the human struggle for love and tries so persistently to be honest about them.

As I have said, the idea of merging with another person comes to the fore in romanticism. That is a primal component in it. Romantic theory also partakes of Platonism, Neoplatonism, sometimes Aristotelianism, and also pantheism—which many scholars have deemed uniquely Romantic: the idea being that passionate love is sacred in itself and therefore justifies one's intense experience; or else, that Romantic love is not just loving someone passionately but may also include a deified version of what Schopenhauer calls "loving-kindness." The latter is not the same as passion.

In Schopenhauer, who was a pessimist and who best represents Romantic pessimism, sexual passion is always an illusion-making device that nature employs to get people to engage in marriage, and therefore coitus, for the sake of reproducing the species. For the men and women who are in love and give themselves to it completely, passion is the greatest thing in life and they are sure it will lead to happiness. In reality, according to Schopenhauer, it is just a cunning self-deception created by nature to get people to procreate. This idea was picked up by Tolstoy and many other writers at the end of the nineteenth century, and also by Freud in the early twentieth century. They thought that passion enables our existence to be affirmative and vibrant, at least bearable, but always severely marred by emotional deception.

Nowadays when people treat Romantic love as the only kind of love, they tend to assume that passionate attachment alone makes life worth living. That is a wholly Romantic idea. It does not exist in the medieval conception of courtly love. In courtly love there may be sex, and even passionate sex—*Tristan and Iseult* is a story of adultery. The troubadours had to avoid that, or pretend to, but the trouvères and other adherents to courtly love didn't fudge the fact that their experience involved carnal indulgence. At the same time, the medieval writers rarely assert that the oceanic feeling of sexual passion justifiably frees one from the bonds of ordinary morality. In the Romantic period, that is exactly what was meant. Passion of this libidinal and erotic sort appears in the glorified abandon and complete yielding of oneself that is then defined as the nature of truly romantic unity between man and woman, and as the basis of all love in general, indeed the only thing that creates meaning and goodness in life.

Bernini's statue of St. Teresa shows her in a state of ecstasy, with her eyes rolling, while she is half-unconscious, or maybe wholly unconscious, but undergoing a passionate love of God. That is how the church was willing to represent religious love—the passionate and total surrender of oneself to the deity. If you take this work of art in isolation from its social setting, let's say if you're a Martian who comes in and looks at that statue, you might see it as something out of *Playboy*. (Well, actually, *Playboy* doesn't show passion. It shows seductiveness. The nude women are not usually in a state of passionate release, but rather experiencing delight and sensuous pleasure designed to arouse *male* passion.) The notion of Romantic love, extolling the supremely passionate, concentrates entirely upon the overwhelming and quasi-religious emotionality that men and women may get from love, particularly sexual love. This view of interpersonal possibilities predominates throughout the history of romanticism in the modern world.

That attitude may also account for the greatly varied acceptability of different objects of love, which is characteristic of our current predilections, above all in our very recent past. The so-called sexual revolution in the 1960s and 1970s was predicated upon the belief that whatever gives you the requisite kicks, whatever excites you very much, is equally good. The concept is an adaptation, or rather modification, of the Romantic belief that by itself and in itself only passion provides the most essential, the most desirable, goodness in life. If so, why should it matter where or how you get the needed stimulus? From this perspective you can also derive the liberation, the acceptability as never before, of homosexual behavior. Across the ages in the Western world, there has been a homophobia that condemns all such inclinations as evil, sick, degenerate, even criminal. Freud refers to homosexuality as an "arrested development." But if passion determines what is good and what makes life worth living, and if you get your passion with a person of the same sex, why should anyone care about his or her gender? It's the passion that matters most.

A significant tie thus exists between gay liberation and the growth of romanticism under the alternate parameters related to differing social conditions. These always come into play, of course. Our erotic and amatory beliefs are not simply ideational. They are also a function of societal, economic, and environmental circumstances. With all that in mind, one can see how the present turmoil about same-sex marriage has its roots in the Romantic upheaval that took place many years ago. Needless to say, its consequences had never been foreseen.

Identification of Love and Passion

In addition to the ones I have mentioned, there are other versions of the Romantic approach to love. While it remained a dominant theme, the identification between love and passion altered from country to country. Whether it may or may not have been typically American, it was very strong in the United States during the twentieth century. In England or Western Europe, and certainly in Eastern Europe or Asia, there existed a somewhat different climate of opinion. Nevetheless, the adoration of passion endures as a touchstone that pervades the varieties of romanticism.

Having said this, I want to emphasize that ideas *alone* never create feelings. And by themselves feelings never amount to ideas, because each of them must be processed cognitively as well as affectively. The two aspects of human nature always interact, but their intersection is so subtle that we often cannot say which is predominant. For some persons in some societies, passion may be a sign of mental illness. Psychotics can be very passionate about things that therapists and other rational people would consider unwholesome. From the point of view of individuals who are healthy but unfulfilled for whatever reason, and then undergo a moment of passion (this is a typical Hollywood script), life can suddenly start to glitter for them. One might occasionally want to say that the before and after ways of life are both sick: the individuals just hadn't been aroused to the degree that a passionate experience awakens, but satisfies only momentarily.

Human beings differ greatly in that respect. Some people don't need much passion. Some need a lot. Most of us have it only in a particular phase of our lives. It's noteworthy that in many marriages—including good marriages—the participants outgrow passion and yet are able to develop into a kind of love that results from having gone *through* the earlier period of passion. Remember that within a lifespan all sorts of physiological changes occur. There are variations in the level of hormones; differences in the strength and deterioration of the body, or if not actual deterioration then alteration in what the body can do; intellectual developments, mental advances or the opposite that one undergoes; and, of course, there is simply the course of daily events that belong to the marital relation itself.

As separate men and women, we all have highly diverse modes of access to life, and sometimes we learn from them. We may even learn how to improve in matters of love. People often fail at this and suffer miseries because they never know what they really want. That would affect the nature of their feelings, the character of their needs for one another, and the kinds of relationships they enter into, which may or may not be passionate. Everyone has a capacity for friendships that, for one reason or another, never issue into passion but can nevertheless be the most rewarding part of a person's life.

The same holds for an individual's art or profession, social involvement, mission as a political force or leader of one's people. Men and women do not have to have much emotionality, and surely not a great deal of romantic passion, in order for those avenues of our existence, those patterns of love, to flourish to some degree or other. To be an ardent teacher does not mean that you seduce your pupils. It means you love the activity of helping them in the ways a teacher can. It has a little, but not very much, to do with sexual romance. Freud would say it's sublimation, and that it always comes down to libidinal frustration or repression. But why? Human nature is extremely broad, and very intricate. There are many social and biological vectors at work within it. I don't think that Freud understood even the biological part, and I see no need to reduce all forms of love to either passionate love or some Romanticized inclination related to it.

In terms of the popular media, you do see massive evidence of a longing for the Romantic. I am not a sociologist, and I don't pretend to know what direction different societies will follow, or how the future in general will compare with what has happened in the past. I have no authoritative knowledge about that. But

I can imagine the affective dimensions in the life that many people lead. I often think about the immediate experience of creative persons. An artist may fall in love with his art. He is driven by a kind of self-love that is wholly appropriate for what he does professionally. He loves himself so much that he learns how to express his being through his technique and through an attachment to, and affection for, the tools of his trade, the materials of his craft, the limiting parameters of his art.

This kind of love explains why a musician lives in terms of sounds. He or she hears them all the time. A painter lives with the emotionality of his pigments. I am a word artist, and much of my active life goes into writing. I am constantly attending to phrases and complete sentences that are meaningful to me. Sometimes the ideas that come forth are not very interesting, yet they are attuned to other ideas, and what matters is the reforming and reshuffling of these concepts throughout the flood of language that flutters within my mind. I spend a lot of time walking by myself. While observing my surroundings, I hear and silently recite words, some of which end up in my prose. It is all a kind of love that cannot be reduced to passionate or romantic love of any kind. Whether or not an artist's experience is thought to be based on narcissism, repression, idealization, or sublimation—though rarely is there a sublimation of anything—it aspires to an aesthetic fulfillment of the human being he or she has become.

At the same time, an artist's love life consists of other affective outlets, some of which involve romantic interests that any person might have, or would like to have, or may have once had. This truism manifests the plurality in our existence. There isn't any one thing that defines us exclusively, and so we inevitably experience different types of love. The job for the philosopher is to help us make our thinking clear about that disparity and to some extent organize it through reasoning, but not in a way that contravenes the reliance upon empirical and naturalistic factuality.

In the course of discussing the ideas of romanticism, my love trilogy includes a lengthy chapter about thinkers whom I call "anti-Romantic Romantics." The three that I deal with most are Kierkegaard, Nietzsche, and Tolstoy. Their views arise from conceptual constructions that were native to nineteenth-century romanticism. They rebel against them and try to supplant the commonplace notions of Romantic love. But in the process they create a new kind of romanticism without which we cannot understand the importance of love as we conceive of it at present. In the case of Nietzsche, the new version articulates his ideas of the superman and of "eternal return," which frequently occur in Romantic theory. And also the notion of "amor fati"—the love of everything, love of all reality. As if human beings can have such a love! As if we know what all of reality might be!

In *Feeling and Imagination*, the more recent book to which I have already referred, I systematically attack the belief that we can even understand what it means to ask what reality is in its totality. In itself this question seems to me indicative of a quasi-religious perspective that some scientists have had (fewer and fewer nowadays) about the basic ability of science, and of properly regulated rational activity in general. It is a faith that seeks to put together all the pieces in the jigsaw puzzle of nature. The assurance it entails is accompanied by the further idea that at some point in the future we will find the solution.

For me what's more pertinent is the anecdote about the computer in *The Hitchhiker's Guide to the Galaxy*. The computer says the meaning of life is 42, and when the investigators are astonished and infuriated by that after generations of waiting for it to provide them with its final answer, the computer replies, "Perhaps your problem is that you don't know what the question means." I agree. We don't really know, and for that reason the Romantic extrapolating to the suggestion that one could have love for everything is grounded in a similar confusion. How *could* we ever know what the "everything" might be? And if we did, how could we possibly have a passionate love that would transcend the obvious limitations in our capacity to love anything?

Though this part of Nietzsche's thinking is typically Romantic, it stems from his rejection of the usual romanticism and a refusal to go back to a pre-Romantic stage, as represented by Kant's philosophy. Kant has a theory of married love in which he talks about joint submission to the personhood of the other individual. Nietzsche says of that: If the two people are always submissive to each other, what is there left between them? Possibly nothing? I think that is very shrewd as a critique of the pre-Romantic attitude about love that Kant exemplifies. But Nietzsche ends up with a type of postromanticism that is even more Romantic than what the Romantics believed, because it tries to extend itself to all there is and to do so in terms of a very mystical and obscure form of cosmic love, very hard for human beings to comprehend, let alone achieve. I will return to this in a later section.

Bestowal and Appraisal in Relation to Freud

To clarify what I have just written, I have to explain the basic structure of my work on love. In the first volume of the love trilogy, I laid a foundation for my future deliberations by distinguishing between appraisal and bestowal. Appraisal: the ability to discover value, in oneself or in other people. Bestowal: a way of creating value, not the same kind of value as in appraisal, but a new kind of value. Bestowal is an engendering of value by means of the relationship we have established, by means of one's appreciative attitude toward the person, thing, or ideal to which we attend. It's a kind of projection. It's a creating of affective value, both in oneself and in the other, which reveals why appraisal alone cannot clarify what love is. Imagine that you have a business relationship in which you get along with your partner and understand his or her nature, and moreover the two of you benefit overtly from each other. But that does not constitute love: you feel and do what you do because you want to get something good out of the other person. While there is nothing wrong in this, it is inherently different from love, which enhances the value of both participants. In bestowal there will always be a concomitant appraisal, but you go beyond appraisal itself and may even disregard it.

Apart from appraisal, no love would exist—we wouldn't even notice what the other is like. At the level of mere appraisal, we are all commodities for each other. And we do experience people at every moment of our lives in terms of some appraisive value we care about. Still, we are able to transcend all that through bestowal without eliminating the unavoidable presence of appraisal. We do so by creating the new kind of relationship that is essential for love.

In the first volume, I argued that Freud didn't understand the nature of bestowal. He thought only in terms of appraisal—the attempt of men and women to benefit from another person as an object of desire. He therefore concluded that love must be the emotional or otherwise affective part of what he saw as pervasive selfishness. He did refer to something that he calls "idealization," which I also discuss at length. But for me idealization is the sheer *making* of ideals. For Freud idealization is an overestimation of some individual, and therefore an illusionary use of appraisal.

According to Freud, love is an *over*valuation that people are prone to enact. In other words, you are bestowing more than the other person is appraisively worth. The lover looks at his girlfriend and thinks she is the most beautiful creature on earth; and if she has a blemish, he loves that too, because it belongs to her. He is thereby employing a distorted appraisal in order to establish excessive value in her, which then becomes the basis of the relationship that comes to exist between them. For Freud all this is just an illusion. In my view, it is Freud who is deluded. He doesn't perceive the character of the lover's more-than-merely-selfish creativity in relation to that other person and whatever blemish he or she may have.

Freud focuses on the fact that many of the people who come to him as patients are suffering because of some Romantic love based on distortions that issue from valuing someone unduly. It blinds them to the fact that the beloved may be aggressive and capable of being destructive, or at least motivated by interests that are inimical. The relationship may therefore be hopeless from the start, and because the afflicted patients have succumbed to this human catastrophe.

I see the situation differently. I too recognize that love may often be a falsification appraisively, and I agree that what Freud says about affective dangers is quite insightful. I don't deny that a good psychiatrist might be able to help a patient overcome this kind of hazard. But as an analysis of the nature of love, the theory Freud introduces is very faulty. Freud was still under the influence of Plato, who didn't care about bestowal but only about a rational use of appraisal in order to understand what mankind, and the world, is like ordinarily. In Freud as in Plato, that approach is a great shortcoming as far as human affect is concerned.

I have never wavered in my belief that Freud has no adequate idea of bestowal. But, in the third volume of *The Nature of Love*, which I wrote many years later than the first, there is a seventy-page chapter on Freud that goes beyond my earlier formulation in the trilogy. By that time, a more thorough reading of his works had revealed to me how wise he frequently is with respect to appraisal. He is clear-minded about the way that people formulate their judgments in affective situations, and how harmful a bad assessment can be. I came to see him as a kind of Jewish mother who says terrible but truthful and accurate things to a son who has fallen hopelessly in love. The son may feel they are hurtful and resulting from a negative bias, even if they are observations that he ought to take seriously. (Incidentally, in referring to a Jewish mother, I don't mean all women who are Jewish and who are mothers, but only the archetype called "the Jewish mother.") Whether or not the association is entirely appropriate to Freud, it's how I began to see him. I admired the perceptiveness embedded in a great many of his remarks—all of them predicated upon his knowledge about the nature of appraisal, though inadequate in relation to bestowal. In that chapter of volume 3, I dealt with Freud's reasoning in a very consecutive manner. I treated him like a fellow philosopher and tried to discover the underlying design in his understanding of appraisal as it contrasts with his lack of comprehension about the nature of bestowal.

Freud is an especially interesting case study because his aspirations and achievements illustrate the more extensive question about the mission of science as a whole and its passionate pursuit of knowledge. Though Freud ended up being largely a literary man, he thought of himself as a scientist and medical specialist throughout his life. His original dream of psychoanalysis was that, in principle, it could all be reduced to physiology or the chemistry in physics. In other words, it might be made into a hard science. He never attained that goal, nor have more recent theorists. Freud's aspiration, however, was wholly scientific. The question remains: What is the role of science—his or anyone else's—in the contemporary world, where its proponents have achieved so much more in the last fifty years, maybe even in the last thirty, than in all prior history? And how can this vast storehouse be applied to the valuational problems of life? How can it have authentic relevance to our emotions and desires, both sexual and amatory?

Since I am myself a literary philosopher, and a humanist, but one who is a naturalist in my general philosophy, I'm entirely amenable to the idea of science being encouraged to continue in its ardent search for truth. I respect all the ways it has succeeded, all the marvels that have come out of it in the form of applied technology. At MIT, where I have taught for many years, I have known the creators of the cognitive revolution that was taking place and is eminently represented by work that people have been doing there. Yet I feel that as good as it is and has become, as important as the work is in itself, and coherent with the exemplary desire to develop much further now that we have access to more powerful tools for investigating the brain than ever before, there remains within the ruling ideology a deficiency not entirely different from what I detected in Freud with respect to bestowal. There is a lack of proper recognition of the role of feelings, of affective realities, that are not wholly amenable to the current modes of investigation.

When cognitive psychologists write about emotion, as they have started to do, they tend to think it can be explained in terms of the rationalistic concepts that science has on hand and that look as if they may suffice. I am convinced this is a fundamental mistake. What one needs is a completely new lexicon and analytic approach to understand the nature of affect, which includes all of what we normally call feelings, emotions, sensations, "intuitive" and "instinctive" dispositions, erotic or libidinal attachments, hatred as well as love, and also kinesthetic impressions of any kind. For that job, we require a totally different type of methodology.

My work on love and sexuality is an effort in this direction. I try to map out the phenomenological blueprint of our affective being. I know that what I have done is incomplete, but possibly it may be of some use to others as time goes by. Throughout *Feeling and Imagination*, which mainly deals with affectivity, I speculate about segments of life that have been neglected by cognitive scientists, indeed by almost everyone except for my kindred spirits in the humanities. I discuss the nature of imagination, of idealization, which differs greatly from the falsifications that Freud had in mind, and of consummation, which is more than just pleasure, but rather our being fulfilled by activities that serve as a payoff for the troubles we go through in developing imagination or idealization. And then there is the underlying aesthetic dimension in life that is surely not reducible to the current parameters of traditional scientific investigation. The truthfulness of a great work of music, let's say, is not the same as scientific truth, and yet one has to find out what it is about aesthetic truth that makes it so essential to the understanding of human existence.

Most of this incipient probing developed in the last ten years or so, after I finished my trilogy entitled *Meaning in Life*. That trilogy consisted of volumes called *The Creation of Value*, *The Pursuit of Love*, and *The Harmony of Nature and Spirit*. In them I talk about values that make us what we are, the search for happiness, what makes life worth living, and above all how the varieties of love actually exist in ordinary experience— not merely the nature of love, but also how the search for it enters into various areas of our life in nature. None of that has yet been dealt with at a philosophical level by any scientist, as far as I know. There does exist excellent, highly commendable, work being done in biology and in neuroscience. But as those fields are envisaged at present, they are limited in scope. They need to be furthered in ways that integrate them with humanistic studies. An adequate philosophy of love for the present age cannot occur without a harmonization of this type.

Schopenhauer and Nietzsche

In considering the prospects for the requisite harmonization, I return to the history of ideas about love, and specifically the work of Nietzsche and Schopenhauer. They have to be studied together. Nietzsche was enamored of Schopenhauer's philosophy when he was young. Schopenhauer died in 1860, so Nietzsche couldn't have known him personally, but having studied his philosophy he considered himself a Schopenhauerian. He glorifies Schopenhauer as the hero of his first book, *The Birth of Tragedy Out of Music*. Schopenhauer's ideas then recur in later books that Nietzsche wrote.

As Nietzsche got older, however, he repudiated more and more details of Schopenhauer's doctrine. He eventually ended up as a critic and not a devotee, which is a healthy development in any philosopher. It is the way that history marches on. Each new generation has to digest the ideas of previous ones, but then progressively eliminate much of what will now seem to them to be excrement. In the case of Nietzsche, his dialectic with Schopenhauer is particularly instructive because it reveals his own weaknesses as well as his unique strength of mind.

For instance, in Nietzsche's final stage of emancipation, he remarks that Schopenhauer called himself a pessimist, which Nietzsche thought confused and counterproductive in various ways—one of which appears in the fact, according to Nietzsche, that Schopenhauer didn't live the life of a pessimist. "Do you know how Schopenhauer spent his day?" he says in effect in one of his later books. "He had a good breakfast, did his writing in the morning, and in the afternoon he went for a walk with his poodle." Incidentally, by the end of his life, Schopenhauer, who lived alone with his dogs, had twenty-four poodles. His lodgings contained photographs of them all on the walls. "After his walk," Nietzsche continues, "Schopenhauer came home, ate a big meal, and then passed the evening playing on the flute. That's not what it is to be a pessimist!"

In response, Schopenhauer would have replied that that's *exactly* what it is to be a pessimist, since if you are one, you don't expect too much of the world, you don't try to live in accordance with very high, remote, wonderful, but unrealistic ideals that nobody can satisfy, and therefore you don't inflict pain upon yourself because of your imperfections. Once you realize that you have fallen short of such ideals, you simply accept yourself as you are and garner pleasures along the way as best you can. You adapt to the reality of this being a world without a God (both Schopenhauer and Nietzsche were atheists), a world without any fundamental meaning and wholly propelled by what later science would call a mere field of energy. There is no prior plan or metaphysical intelligence to be deciphered. Existence is a function of what Schopenhauer called the

"Will," by which he meant the dynamic force in nature itself.

The outlines of this view were accepted by Nietzsche as much as by Schopenhauer. The latter believed that if you're a pessimist you can adjust to the situation much better than if you're an optimist. Of course, he couldn't comment on the experience of Nietzsche, who wasn't yet born when Schopenhauer formulated his philosophy. But one can extrapolate and say that if Schopenhauer had met his quasi disciple, he would have said to Nietzsche, "But you've lived such an unhappy life" (which is true), "you've suffered so much, sometimes because of psychosomatic illness, and all this results from your optimistic pursuit of elevated but fruitless ideals."

The noblest of them I touched on when I mentioned the concept of amor fati. According to Nietzsche, that consists in accepting everything as it is, in loving everything simply because it is what it happens to be. It is a dictum he could never have learned from Schopenhauer, who taught that life is tragic, since the meaningless Will uses us as pawns just for the sake of enabling it to go on existing in some respect—in our case, through reproduction of the human species. Schopenhauer was convinced there is no reason to love indiscriminately that or any other mode of reality. The

Will is hideous; it's horrible, he insisted, and our life in each instance and its totality is just a trivial byproduct. Thus spake Schopenhauer, but Nietzsche condemned him as a naysayer.

For Schopenhauer the question of suicide has special significance within his system of thought. He argues against it in a somewhat convoluted manner. He claims that the Will doesn't want to foster the existence of people who are defeated in life and therefore incapable of beneficially creating the next generation. The person who wishes to commit suicide is clearly a loser. He has been crushed by the hardships of survival in the world, and so the Will is delighted, so to speak, to get rid of him. Not being alive, the Will doesn't have intelligence or feeling but merely manifests what is advantageous to its own continuance. From that point of view, suicide fits perfectly into the scheme of things. It eliminates people who are so incapable of mastering life that nothing but harm can come from letting their genes get into the species' gene pool. Suicide succeeds in dispensing with them, and that is what the Will "wants." According to Schopenhauer, our salvation as human beings occurs in repudiating the Will. *Because* it is cruel and without value in itself, a person can obtain a sense of dignity and self-respect only by refusing to accept it. Therefore, Schopenhauer concludes, suicide is not a valid solution.

Schopenhauer delineates several paths of salvation. Each of them is a way of saying No! to the Will. You decline to play the game. One might reply that it is the person who commits suicide who is really refusing to play the game. And if he acts because of enlightened awareness (because he has studied and admired Schopenhauer's philosophy), or because he is courageous and understands the world well enough to repudiate the Will in this emphatic though metaphysical sense, isn't he or she on the way to salvation?

Schopenhauer rejects that kind of reasoning. He says that any man or woman who cannot cope with life is not on the path of salvation. Schopenauer is against suicide for everybody, including those who might or might not be seeking salvation. To someone who considers suicide, he says: If you kill yourself—let's say you're very unhappy and you're walking in the mountains and you find yourself on a precipice and have a feeling that you would like to throw yourself over—if you act on that impulse, you will just be doing what the Will wants you to do. But you ought to be defeating the Will and not foolishly acquiescing in it under any circumstances.

This concept of nay-saying is very crucial in the development of Schopenhauer's ideas about how to live a good life and attain at least a modicum of happiness.

Though Nietzsche did not disagree with Schopenhauer's premises, he maintains that we have to learn how to say Yes! to nature. This, however, poses a major problem in Nietzsche's thought. Isn't he too a naysayer insofar as he also believes that life is tragic and that nature has no interest in what happens to mere pawns like us? You would assume so. But if he advocates saying yes to the Will and enjoying life by living with a love of everything—evil as it all is—he seems to be moving in a different and contradictory direction. Nietzsche says we must affirm nature as the "superman" does. The superman is a person who is able to master the Will, to fulfill nature, and to flourish in it. The only example of a superman that he really depicts in his writing is not a Hitlerian kind of monster but rather the artist. A true artist, he asserts, learns how to love and be creative in relation to all of nature.

This split between Schopenhauer and Nietzsche has very wide ramifications—and not only in terms of one's ability to love. But before I expand on that, let me note how divergent is their thinking about love. In his major book *The World as Will and Representation*, Schopenhauer includes a long and fascinating chapter sometimes translated into English as "The Metaphysics of Love Between the Sexes" and at other times as "The Metaphysics of Sexual Love." He argues there that poets have spoken the truth when they called love the most important thing in life. Modern cynics who say love really doesn't matter that much are out of touch, he states, since love is the *most* fundamental part of life. The trouble with both the cynics and the idealistic poets, Schopenhauer claims, is that they don't understand love's metaphysical function, how it operates in reality. Since the Will is directed only toward preserving itself biologically, human feeling and behavior must ultimately be explained in terms of love, which for Schopenhauer basically means sex.

Freud acquired that idea from him. In his book *Beyond the Pleasure Principle*, written in 1923, Freud acknowledges as much. He remarks that without knowing it, he seems to have steered his ship into the port of Schopenhauer's metaphysics. He gleaned his conception of sex at an early age from reading Schopenhauer. Not being a philosopher himself, Freud used Schopenhauer's writings as a prelude to theoretical analyses that are primarily scientific. On the other hand, for Schopenhauer the science of biology itself provides the clue to what is essential in his metaphysics. So the two thinkers are very much alike in that respect.

Schopenhauer says that love is a device for getting the right man and woman to have sexual intercourse that will bring about the next generation. He also recognizes, but not as clearly as a contemporary ethologist or behavioral biologist would, that there is the additional necessity of protecting and preserving the next generation. This too is part of the process of reproduction, and hence the fundamental reality of love as Schopenhauer sees it. He explains all apparent idealism in these terms, including what I would call the bestowal of value, and also what Freud interprets as overvaluation of the object. In Schopenhauer's view, love is just nature's contrivance for getting people to engage in whatever coital pattern that is needed. The man becomes attached to a woman because he falls in love with her. What goes along with that is the bestowing of value, idealizing her as the most beautiful person in the neighborhood, maybe in the world; and it's the same thing reciprocally in the woman's attitude toward the man. But all of this is based on illusion, Schopenhauer insists, since both persons are being systematically manipulated by nature's supervening will-to-live.

Implications for Marriage

In making that assertion, Schopenhauer hooks onto the common, very long-standing, cynical view about love that maintains it is always blind, and that people in love are unable to use their reason. There may be a partial truth in this idea and yet, as I argue, it also harbors a major misconception. It fails to recognize that love is never entirely illusory. A relationship that partakes of love is, to that extent, creative. If a painter looks at a canvas and says that such and such colors would be good next to each other, there is no illusion in his belief. And the same thing happens in human sexual or amatory situations. Emphasis upon bestowal and the creativity in love takes one beyond the cynical notion that claims it is detrimental and inherently deficient. Schopenhauer dignifies this idea because he thinks it provides a good biological explanation for the fact that the glittering falsities of love encourage people to get married and to engage in reproductive sex as often as they do.

In a different period of history, in a different society, Schopenhauer might have recognized that you don't have to get married for that, or you can have any number of wives, as in Islam. (Not nowadays, since at present polygamy is usually limited to three or four wives, but many men had more in earlier Muslim cultures.) Schopenhauer lived in nineteenth-century bourgeois Germany, and he was thinking of conventional marriage in the West as part and parcel of the standard procedure for continuing the species. In order to get people to get married, he thought, they had to have a prior period of falling in love when they would be suitably fooled by their ideas about the perfection of the other person. Once they do get married, Schopenhauer states, all the happiness they thought they were going to have in uniting with this particular man or woman will disappear. The children having been thrust into the world, the former lovers will end up hating or ignoring each other.

There is, however, a qualification to this negative stance that Schopenhauer allows. He remarks that the primal course of marriages can be redirected, in the sense that they need not always be predicated upon sexual ardor. The illusory phase comes from passionate romantic feelings, but you can get married without any of those. That happens in a marriage of convenience. An old man who doesn't have much sexual energy might marry a charming young woman who will take good care of him and feed him well. She can be devoted to him for whatever reason, perhaps because she wants to inherit his wealth, but that won't matter. They could live in perfect happiness with each other, and even if they are separated by age and physical capacity, they might have a good relationship. This is in principle what some people recommend nowadays as the only acceptable type of love. It is called "companionate marriage." The spouses ideally accept each other as lifelong companions, and, it is argued, this can bring about the greatest probability of happiness, which evades those powerful sexual feelings that make people hostile and dissatisfied and therefore unable to live together in peace.

In my essay "Marriage: Same-Sex and Opposite-Sex" (2004), I used the example of George Bernard Shaw and his wife to illustrate a sexless marriage. It was not entirely blissful, but it managed all right. It was a working arrangement for forty-five years until she died. They both had professional interests of their own, and they lived together in a harmonious manner. That fits the conception of companionate marriage. Schopenhauer would probably cite it as an example of a union that is not based on sexual need, sexual immersion, or sexual passion that nature instills in us together with illusory hopes of happiness, which are often defeated later on. This other kind of marriage, the kind that is capable of lasting and being satisfactory, Schopenhauer does not debunk at all. He thinks it's a viable possibility. It may not always lead to actual happiness, he says, but it is more likely to do so than if you marry for love.

There are various consequences of this view that Schopenhauer doesn't investigate and that nobody has written much about. I have made some peripheral attempts along these lines, but more can be done on the basis of the work I did in the *Nature of Love* trilogy. For instance, one could study Schopenhauer in the context of what eighteenth-century thinkers like David Hume wrote or, even earlier, Michel Montaigne and others in France. They believed that there are two kinds of love. One of them is sexual love, and that is usually very powerful. Hume and Montaigne see nothing essentially wrong with it under any circumstances. It can be adulterous, or premarital, or what a single man or woman does who never gets married but has love affairs—a panorama of arrangements not entirely different from what has frequently existed in recent generations.

But Hume insists that this is only part of the story, since sexual love can readily issue into kindliness, what Schopenhauer would call loving-kindness. That is a type of concern about a person's welfare as well as admiration of whatever goodness for yourself that you might find in him or her, apart from the libidinal desire you feel toward this individual. Hume's analysis of sexual love has three components that can sometimes be united: sexual fervor, love of beauty in the other person, and a kindly disposition toward that man or woman. I believe it is a very fertile and interesting analysis of the nature of sexual love.

Though these criteria may be satisfied in passionate love affairs of a nonmatrimonial sort, Hume also says, marriage can provide something else. It can create a family as a unit in society, it can yield a great deal of the comfort you get from someone who is your partner in the marital venture and who issues from a family different from your own but now allied to it. With that other person you also share economic and social interests that matter to you both. None of this is directly based upon sexual impulse.

You have a choice between these two modalities of love, Hume tells us. There is, or can be, happiness, even joy, in the purely sexual relations, but they are frequently tumultuous, above all if they exist in a society that does not approve of them. You then incur a penalty for savoring such delights. On the other hand, there are goods to be gained from a companionate marriage that make it a superior type of attachment, provided it is truly harmonious. Nevertheless it will not be all-consuming, as a powerful sexual affair might become. Libidinal passion would probably be excluded most of the time, and sexual pleasure in general may be diminished. Hume concludes that the love and happiness of a good marriage differs entirely from what belongs to falling in love, or even carnal love of any kind. He leaves it for each reader to decide which alternative is preferable.

Dualism and Freud on Erotic Degradation

In the twentieth century various philosophers have made comparable analyses in terms of a distinction between what José Ortega y Gasset calls "true love" and "falling in love." In classic Spanish fashion, Ortega describes true love as inherently related to marriage. It is an institutional state of living with somebody without necessarily having much of the fervor or sensuous pleasure that belongs to falling in love. In itself love involves a form of feeling that is unlike that, he thinks, and very remote from passion as a whole. So there again we find the dualism that is built into the structure of Hume's philosophy of love.

At this point we may turn to a related analysis that Freud offers in a brilliant essay, called in one translation "The Most Prevalent Form of Degradation in Erotic Life." Another title appears in other books of Freud, but it's the same essay. His idea is that patients—male patients—often come to him, complaining that while they are very virile, capable of enjoyable sexual performance with their mistress, they are impotent with their spouse. That troubles them, mainly because it's upsetting to the wife, who cannot find satisfaction elsewhere, given the fact that nineteenth-century Viennese society expected women to remain faithful to their husbands. Without causing a scandal, wives could not go out and get a lover the way husbands did in having successive mistresses.

The patients presented the problem to Freud from their point of view as husbands. Like many of the other pathologies that Freud encountered, especially in his early practice, this one results from the difficulty of living in a world that was dominated by concepts of Romantic love within the marital culture prevalent at the time. To some degree, Freud was confronting not so much biological reality, but rather ideological mandates as defined by the nature of social mores in a cosmopolitan city like Vienna and in relation to the two stages of romanticism that I have mentioned—the benign and the pessimistic.

Freud's way of stating the situation is wonderfully succinct. He says about these men, "Where they can lust, they cannot love, and where they can love, they cannot lust." In answer to his questioning whether they love their wife, the men generally say, in my paraphrase, "I do love my wife, and I want to be able to perform sexually with her." "Do you love your mistress?" Freud would then ask, and they would reply, "No, it's not love; I have love for my wife, but the other woman is merely attractive sexually. I enjoy her physically and I'm perfectly capable of satisfying that aspect of my nature in the process. It's just that I love only my wife." This whole idea that you love a wife but do not love a mistress with whom you have good sex is typical of nineteenth-century romanticism. It's based on some of the misleading concepts that I try to rectify in my philosophy of love.

For me love is something that can happen in any number of different, pluralistic, ways. You may not love your girlfriend exactly as you love you wife, but you can love both simultaneously. Neither love is the same as your love for apple pie or a beautiful painting or musical composition, or your country, or God if you are religious. These are all different kinds of love that have to be understood in terms of their own variability and their own individual dimensions. But the one that trumped all the rest in the nineteenth century was Romantic love, particularly as directed toward a person of the opposite sex and, customarily, in terms of a satisfying sexual relationship.

Freud doesn't tell us very much about his therapy for the men's dilemma. He gets them to talk about it and to recognize that the nature of their anguish lies in the fact that they can lust where they cannot love and love where they cannot lust. In other words, the sheer separation between loving and lusting is the cause of their suffering. We post-Freudians have learned this lesson, and nowadays the two attitudes are often unified in the popular imagination. Most people in the West don't think of romantic love as being puristic anymore. We think of it as somehow related to sex, much as Freud taught at the beginning of the twentieth century. But he didn't teach the lesson well enough, I'm convinced, though we are all dominated by his formulations just the same.

In my estimation, Freud made a number of errors, to which I allude in various books. Without enumerating these errors here, I single out one that is especially egregious—his belief in the *primacy* of sexual motivation—the idea that even the most apparently sexless attachment must be based on, at least explicable in terms of, sex as a biological force that permeates virtually all human response. In a sense, this may be true. Almost every person wants to meet someone, usually of the opposite sex, with whom he or she can enjoy complete and gratifying libidinal experiences, not just holding hands in the moonlight. But it does not follow that love, all the varieties of love, can be reduced to an overt or inherent desire for consummatory sex. Our modern confusion about that is related to the thinking of Freud.

Though Freud was speaking as a therapist and a medical man in the essay I just cited, it is also particularly interesting as sociology. He points out very shrewdly that the women his patients married were likely to belong to the same upper stratum of society as they did. These were people who were well off financially; they could not have gone to a doctor like Freud if they weren't. They were members of the middle class, the upper middle class, and the upper class itself, and they married women who were like themselves in that respect. This meant that there were three types of womanhood that were jointly represented in the marital situation of these men—the wife, the mother, and the sister. They all existed in a circumscribed level of society, and the mother might even have picked the bride, or at least encouraged her son to marry her. In any event, the man's mother and his sisters would be symbolic of the female niche in which the wife would now have a prearranged role. And so, to a large degree, the emotional problem was also a societal one. The patients are persons who cannot respond sexually to women who belong to the small circle from which they could choose a legitimate wife. Then, of course, there are the psychoanalytic ideas about a man's love for his mother, or the affectionate love he may have for a sister, that belong to Freud's general theory and that issue into the sociological approach he elaborates in his essay.

We came upon this in the present discussion because the Freudian perspective is at its base an extension of

Schopenhauer's views about love as sex, as well as his assertion that you can have a good and loving marriage without the sexual passion that the Will subtly steers you toward—in other words, what is called a marriage of reason that can provide family happiness even if it is devoid of the libidinal consummations you may find in the arms of someone else. That common dualism of the seventeenth and eighteenth centuries underlies the experience of the men who go to Freud for his help and whom Freud analyses with this bifurcation in mind. Freud himself complained that society was too severe with people who faced such problems. Either they had love affairs only and never married, or else they felt compelled to have adulterous relationships. In either event, they reached beyond the comfortable nineteenth-century mold of heterosexual monogamous marriage and were often punished as a result.

In saying what he does, Freud speaks explicitly as a political or moral advocate of changes in the social order. He's not just talking as a therapist or theorist of love and sex. His outlook reveals how the doctrine that Schopenhauer had developed in his philosophy filtered into later thought and practice. Freud is a dualist in many aspects. In my contrasting analyses, starting with my ideas about bestowal and appraisal, I struggle to see what would be a nondualistic, and possibly more accurate, resolution of these questions.

The issue of love in marriage goes back to the Book of Genesis. The ideality of it is often invoked in the Old Testament: that people might marry because of love, and having married they would indeed be able to love and remain true to each other. The association between love and marriage is therefore not new. But what differed in the nineteenth century and the beginnings of the twentieth, and to some degree remains today, is the general ideology, the philosophical groundwork, that goes with the Romantic view of marriage and love as a whole. We are trying still to deal with that, though by the end of the twentieth century many people had repudiated all forms of nineteenth-century romanticism. This in turn derived from the anti-Romantic revolution, which began about 1900. It contested any type of idealism that lends itself to a Romantic formulation.

Hegel, the great philosopher of "objective idealism," had been a close affiliate of the poet Friedrich Hölderlin, an important figure in German Romantic theorizing. One could in fact interpret Hegel's phenomenology as a philosophical version of what would later flourish as Romantic poetry. Creative

writers throughout the West—Coleridge, for example—
got a great deal out of Schelling, whose ideas were
similar to Hegel's. It's a form of idealism inasmuch as
the entire world is thought to be striving for perfection,
history not being a product of material development
but rather a dialectic of aspiring mental states that
progressively bring about changes in our experience of
the physical world.

Marx altered the overall conception by saying that
the evolving ideals are themselves an outcome of
material and technological developments in the human
interaction with the realm of matter. This controversy
is largely a family quarrel between Hegel and followers
of his like Marx. But even in Marx, there was a vision
of the ideal future, which is for him utopian commu-
nism, not what people in the Soviet Union ever attained,
or thought they could attain, or were really trying to
attain. At the same time, the pervading espousal of
idealism remained constant, whether you were a
dialectical materialist like Marx or a dialectician of
ideas like Hegel. All that arose out of the Romantic
attitude toward life and its philosophy of love.

Post-Romantic variations beyond romanticism
proper, or the conflict between the poles of benign and
pessimistic romanticism as I distinguish them, were
developmental offshoots of the Romantic worldview.

By the twentieth century its opponents sought to demolish romanticism completely, just as they tried to eradicate the philosophy of objective idealism. Nevertheless, both linger on in the present. Various elements of each have survived and even gone much further than anyone could have predicted. One of these components is relevant to the idea of democracy.

Democracy as Related to Romanticism

Democracy as we know it is a product of the late eighteenth century and, above all, the French and American revolutions. Thus it overlaps with romanticism. The ideal of modern democracy is that each person has a right to pursue his or her own happiness in his or her own way, even selfishly and in self-oriented activities that mean most to that person alone. But in that case, why should young people marry or seek a sexual partner because of the social class that either individual comes from, or in conformity with the preference of their parents? Why shouldn't they be allowed to behave freely in terms of their feelings, for whatever purpose and for any erotic motive? In romanticism, feeling was the most important part of human nature, whereas in the eighteenth century, reason was—as the long tradition going back to Plato thought it should be. Modern democracy can therefore be seen as a manifestation of the Romantic attitude.

Even so, the quest for social and affective applications of democracy has outlived romanticism and has now been extended throughout the world in regions that sometimes had little prior experience of Romantic theorizing, or its ups and downs in the West. If you think democratically, the usual barriers to personal liberty are destroyed. Men and women are permitted to look for happiness in their own fashion, and no one is entitled to tell them who in particular must be their heart's delight, or even that this person has to belong to the opposite gender. The recent agitation about a legal right to same-sex relations is a consequence of the democratic spirit that began to blossom at the beginning of the nineteenth century. It is opposed by people who either come from other traditions—Catholicism, for instance—or are concerned about the future of the family and worry about its being undermined by such liaisons, basically because of the deviant sexual tie but also by the prospect of that becoming legitimized through the honorific bond of marriage. This is the crux of the heated debates that are now going on in the United States and in some other countries.

In America the ferment issued from the liberalization that took place during the Vietnam War. Various incursions upon sexual freedom were washed away by the social movements that became prominent in the 1960s and 1970s. In wartime there often is some relaxing of sexual and personal restraints. Having lived through the Second World War, I know firsthand that the American soldiers in England were able to enjoy intimate relations with compliant English girls that would not have been allowed under any other circumstances. During the Vietnam War something similar occurred abroad and among people back home in the United States. There was an easing of sexual repressiveness simply because it was a time of crisis and the young had to be accorded more freedom to do what they wanted.

What many of them wanted was to parade nude or have communes or engage in sexual orgies with anyone they fancied. After that, a reaction set in and everything became much more circumscribed. But the very fact that the so-called sexual revolution took place when it did in a democratic country remained as a precedent that then spilled over to the forbidden area of sexual orientation, "the love that dare not speak its name," as Oscar Wilde called it, which is homosexual love. It was given a chance to liberate itself a little at first, and now very strongly.

I see this entire development as a derivation out of romanticism in the modern world. It is romanticism in

relation to sociological and political conditions inter-
woven with the democratic spirit. For its part, democracy in the United States is closely united to globalization,
which is extremely pervasive nowadays. Our desire
to spread democracy throughout the world doesn't
happen just by chance. The two vectors are part of the
same socioeconomic mindset as it has unfolded in
different places and in different decades. If you have a
form of life, like democracy, that applies throughout
the world, it is beneficial to globalize corporations and
have free trade in virtually every country. These things
go together, though not in a deterministic way. Their
occurrence is often very unpredictable, and there are
often contradictory phases.

There never is a straight-line progression in a history
of this kind. There are always remnants of the past and
forces that are moving in alternate directions toward a
future that is inevitably unrealized in some respect or
other. It's a little like an army traveling through foreign
terrain. If you represent its advance on a map and chart
where a regiment or brigade is currently, you may see
little fingers emerge, and sometimes the fingers get cut
off because that segment of the army has been encircled
by the enemy and cannot reform itself. A comparable
type of dynamic, and unforeseeable, actuality exists in
the economic, social, and political aspects of love and

sexuality that I have been depicting. In the mapping of these affective coordinates, everything occurs in a flux of permanent contingency not unlike a military operation.

Even among like-minded revolutionary thinkers, there is frequently great variance in their views about love and sex. Though Marx was an intellectual rebel, he was very conservative in his ideas about the commendable union of man and woman. He seems to have had a happy marriage, and he naturally envisaged married love on the basis of his own experience. While his meditations in this area are of interest, they are not as interesting as the writings of Engels, his close associate. Engels never got married, as a matter of principle. He had theories about human affect that were much more radical than those of Marx. The USSR tried to combine the views of both.

In some respects the official position was very straitlaced. Stalin did not want the comrades wandering too far afield, for fear that they might end up becoming degenerate like people in the West, where there was free love and all that implies. At the same time, various aspects of Soviet society were quite liberated. You could get married in front of any justice of the peace. If you then wanted to get divorced, you had only to send in a postcard, and that was the end of that. It was a kind of liberation that came with a sense of danger and upheaval, and of course the Soviet Union, though it lasted seventy years, was most of the time very fearful of outside invasion and internal chaos. The mentality I mentioned as relevant to America's Vietnam War operated there as well. People had access to more sex and more experimentation in love as well as sex just because everything was in such turmoil. That would bring personal conduct closer to the thinking of Engels, in contrast to the more static attitude of someone like Stalin, who wanted to control men and women so that the government could use them for its political purposes.

Existentialism

If we now move on to twentieth-century existentialism, we find that Jean-Paul Sartre is its most impressive philosopher of love. In his earliest writings he had a negative view about affective relations, but in his last works he became somewhat more affirmative. Sartre went through three stages, the first of which is presented in *Being and Nothingness*. He talks there about love and sex as a futility. "Man is futile," he says. One reason he cites is the fact that people want to be loved by someone who will treat them as an absolute source of meaningfulness. Through this mode of acceptance, the lover would somehow take possession of the other person. That alone inevitably causes emotional friction, according to Sartre. Throughout all his writings you get the idea of interpersonal conflict, which he considers inherent in our nature. In one place at the end of his life, he said, "What I've known most in my life is conflict, and the fact that conflict is fundamental in human relations."

Above all, Sartre thinks this unavoidable struggle is always built into the structure of intimate, sexual, amatory relationships. The lover wants to possess the beloved's being, he says, while the beloved is submitting to that in an attempt to possess the being of the lover. The model for this conception is Hegel's parable about the slave and the master. The master becomes the slave of the slave by virtue of his very hunger for masterhood. Sartre's approach ends up in a pervasive skepticism about all interhuman efforts to find happiness. He finally asserts that the reason man is, and must be, a futility results from wanting to be God even though no God exists.

That's the burden of Sartre's early philosophy. Later his thinking changed, largely because of Simone de Beauvoir. In her book *The Ethics of Ambiguity* she gets far beyond what Sartre wrote in *Being and Nothingness*, and she constantly points him in the direction of a more humanistic view of mankind's possibilities. The last years of Sartre's life were given to a number of unfinished works. His thinking became more and more Marxist, but he never completed his massive writings of that sort. He barely finished his multivolume book on Flaubert. And also he kept working on an endless ethical philosophy that was supposed to remedy the defects in *Being and Nothingness* as he came to recognize them, particularly in the area of social and affective relations. He called the opus *Cahiers pour une morale* (*Notebooks for an Ethics*), but he died without being fully satisfied with what he had accomplished. It remained as a bundle of preliminary notes, and often not very intelligible ones since they were only jottings that he wrote down over a period of time.

As usual with Sartre, however, the hodgepodge manuscript was very lengthy. He gave it to his literary executor and told her that he didn't want to publish the book himself because it clearly needed more work, but that when he died she could do with it whatever she wished. So after his death she immediately had it published. Trying to make my way through this discursive morass, I thought it was fascinating, perhaps because there were many ideas that seemed similar to my own. It articulates a type of humanistic, pluralistic, empirical approach, though only through germs of thought that Sartre was never able to solidify despite his desire to move beyond *Being and Nothingness*.

There is one issue in the *Cahiers* that especially intrigued me. It was carried further in a perceptive way by Robert C. Solomon, who studied Sartre's views with great understanding. In his own fashion, Solomon articulates ideas about the nature of the love relationship that are related to Sartre's, and which I don't agree with in either case. It's a question about freedom and autonomy. Everyone wants to have autonomy, and yet people also want to bind themselves to others. They want to be intimate, even though intimacy with someone else means sacrificing one's freedom in some regard. Consequently, there results a dialectical tension, as Sartre and Solomon put it, between both wanting to be bound up and wanting to be totally free, although these are contradictory. We are all concerned about our own welfare, which involves our freedom, and this is jeopardized when we enter into a situation of close interdependence with another person since the relationship ineluctably entails self-abnegation and may even threaten our own individuality.

Sartre poses that dilemma as a deep ontological split in human nature. He thinks of love as always being a function of this fundamental divisiveness.

Solomon picks up that point of view and develops a similar outlook. What particularly interested me about the thinking of both was the ambiguous approach to the question of merging that they have in common. At least in Sartre's version, but also in the terminology that Solomon recurrently uses, the intimacy that is threatened by the will to retain one's cherished freedom, thereby causing the conflict, the ambiguity, the tension, is an intimacy that has been envisaged as a kind of merging. Since I deny that merging is definitive of love, I am unconvinced by the overall phenomenology that Sartre and Solomon try to construct. Moreover, I don't think the human search for freedom is itself correctly analyzed by Sartre. As I argue in *The Pursuit of Love*, autonomy and freedom are totally different.

An early discussion by Sartre about our need to be free is worth mentioning in this context. Throughout *Being and Nothingness*, he returns to the danger, as well as the profound significance, of what he calls "the look." He says that if someone looks at you there is something in the look itself that embodies an attempt to possess you. By looking at someone, you make that other person into an object of your observation and appropriation. I criticize this idea in the third volume of my love trilogy, in a lengthy chapter on theological as well as atheistic existentialism. It deals mainly with

Sartre and de Beauvoir, but existentialists like Martin
Buber and Gabriel Marcel also come into it. In relation
to Sartre, I maintain that his concept of the look is
untenable, because it ignores what is called the "look
of love"—as in the famous song by Burt Bacharach—or
a mother's tenderness in looking at her child as she
does, gazing at the offspring with devotion and protec-
tiveness. That kind of look need not imply possessive-
ness or anything like appropriation. It can express
acceptance and even adoration instead. Though I was
still approaching love as bestowal and appraisal in this
stage of my analysis, my later ideas about love as an
"accepting" of another person are also pertinent.

I think the same critique applies to the emotional
tension in terms of which Sartre defines romantic love
as a whole. In his final writings—the *Cahiers* above
all—his treatment of the intimacy in erotic love seems
to me unfortunate since it presupposes a kind of oneness
that is extraneous to the way in which each accepts
the other as he or she is. Similarly, Sartre's notion of
autonomy is faulty because that need not be based
upon any striving to take possession of someone's
freedom. It may only be a desire to share a state of
interdependence with him or her. My discussion leads
into related ideas of mine about love as a sharing of
selves, which run counter to Sartre's views in the last

phase of his philosophy as well as the first. *The Pursuit of Love* includes a detailed presentation of these further ideas.

In a symposium on my philosophy of love, a specialist on existentialism agreed with most of what I said but charged there was one aspect of Sartre's approach that I neglected. He was referring to Sartre's sociological and political investigations, which underlie his philosophy of love. This critique seems to me correct, and I accept it as a fair complaint to be made against my writing. Though John Dewey's books about politics and society had a great influence on me, I have always regretted that I could not emulate his achievement in that field. At the same time, I knew that when it comes to the philosophy of love or sex, Dewey says next to nothing. I therefore tended to think that if only I could supplement what he did by adding what I was capable of attaining in the areas he ignored, I would end up with a more comprehensive philosophy than his. It's like the Jewish joke about the peddler, the poor man, who says that if he had the wealth of Rothschild, he'd be richer than Rothschild. When someone asks, "How is that possible?" the peddler answers, "I'd also hold onto my own money." In other words, I felt that, in my intellectual poverty, I might be able to increase my modest talent with the vast assets of Dewey (or

Sartre). But, of course, the notion is ludicrous: wisdom does not come from mere accretion, and anyhow we all have to learn how to live with our personal limitations.

A little more comment on Sartre's belief in the unavoidability of tension may be helpful here. We human beings want both independence and valid oneness with others but we can't have both, he insists, and therefore our search for love must always remain in a state of constant vacillation. Or, I suppose, he would call it metaphysical anxiety, the very nature of the amatory enterprise having that effect. As a result, Sartre sees no exit from our predicament. He does not and cannot imagine a plausible resolution of the interpersonal conflict he describes.

In a sense, I don't begrudge that failure on Sartre's part. It is not the job of philosophers to offer final solutions to any of the massive questions about our being. Mathematicians can solve problems, and sometimes with great mastery in the eloquence and certitude of their proofs, but the doing of philosophy is something else. Philosophers help by making important ideas a little clearer than before. At their best, they provide a challenging and novel vista upon the world. In the process they might elicit both criticism and approval from people who are willing to think about what has been argued. Future generations may go on to develop, in some manner and to some degree, whatever they garner from the challenging views. They may even use them to learn for themselves how to live. But there is no ultimate resolution to be achieved.

In keeping with my belief that philosophy is an art form like any other, I've never pretended to solve anything conclusively. I've never sought to approximate a scientific description of love or sex, or anything else. Neither have I tried to give a formal delineation of love and sex. As I keep repeating, I don't believe these enormous categories of thought are amenable to strict definitions or comprehensive solutions. There is an open texture to the nature of love, compassion, friendship, sex, and all the other relations that people value highly. Profound ambiguities reside in these matters and philosophers can and should address them, but it would be foolish to think that any analysis or description that has value can be neatly enclosed in precise formulations, especially the ones that presuppose necessary and sufficient conditions.

If you are a philosopher, you can only make a personal portrait that may be true to yourself, to your times, to your style of thought or writing, and thereby proffer imaginative and possibly genuine insights into the nature of human experience. If what you write is both lucid and suggestive, it may excite the imagination of other people, and that's marvelous. If it doesn't, you have to face the daunting prospect of your work as a conceptual artist falling stillborn from the press. Like "ole' man river," the world will just keep on rolling along. You have to keep up with it if you can, but never say to yourself, "I've finally solved the ultimate problems of life (whatever they may be)."

The Love of Life: A Pluralist Perspective

There is a paragraph in a book by William James in which he remarks (in my paraphrase), "I've been trying to present you with a new way of thinking and to bring up approaches to various issues that I hope you will want to consider. If they don't interest you, if they don't speak to your soul, if they're not really as important for you as they are for me, forget about them, throw my book away!" I find something very American about that—here is the commodity and, if you'll pay money for it, if it is salable on the market, if it'll fly in Peoria, as they say, and have an appeal to a large and receptive audience, then that's fine. If not, discard it! James pulls off the notion in a comical fashion, which often happens in his writings.

These Jamesian remarks may seem to some readers like a byproduct of American capitalism, even though James was liberal in his politics and was not an apologist for big business or the idea that philosophy is *just* another commodity to be bought and sold. He believed that to get beyond the marketplace, you have to live your intellectual life with faith in yourself, with courage, with something like the amor fati that Nietzsche was talking about but without the assumption that you can stretch it into a love of *everything*.

Nietzsche goes too far. Did he expect us to love the periodic table in chemistry or the laws of thermody-namics, or the explosions that are taking place in remote galaxies, or even in our own galaxy and on our sun? I see no hope of explaining love that way; the notion doesn't make any sense to me. But the idea of indiscriminately loving other human beings and other species, the idea of loving the love that all living creatures do or want to feel for themselves, their *love of love*, that means a great deal to me. If you have this kind of love and live your life with it as your motiva-tion, approaching your individual predilections with something comparable to a painter's love of his materials, his experience, and maybe his models, that suffices whether or not you are a philosopher. Future generations may remember you, or they may forget both you and what you cared about. What matters most is doing what you can for the sake of living most fully in the present, while you are still active and in command of your faculties.

Only by exercising a vital effort of this type can you love the life in others and in yourself. It is not surprising to me that Dewey lived to be ninety-three—which was a very old age when he died in 1952. Many of the great philosophers, several of them in the modern period, had long and fruitful careers. It is the vital involvement—the consecutive use of one's mind and body, living life with love and dedication—that enables such people to go on. Dewey believed that the good life is like climbing from one mountain range to another; and when there are no more ranges, you die. The point is that by being creative in your work and in your experience you attain a love of life that keeps you alive. The world may give you a horse laugh if you expire suddenly! It is nevertheless a worthy motive and rational principle to retain as best one can.

At the same time, we have to give serious attention to Sartre's emphasis upon the unavoidable separateness between human beings. It seems radically incompatible with love. If true, Sartre's scruple undermines all personal relationships and the making of any sacrifices for another individual or some unselfish cause. At the same time, what Sartre argues is correct and wholly appropriate to the sense of

isolation and even alienation that many people experience nowadays in our mechanized societies. Our world
is moving into a reconstruction that will create new
values that are very different from the old ones. But
that has been the case as long as civilizations have
been evolving as they do, and we need not despair
completely. Sartre's all-encompassing pessimism is
surely unfounded.

There have always been laments about the passing
of the "good old days," and how everything is going
to pieces now. I remember feeling that way about
technology in my youth. I discuss the matter in *Three
Philosophical Filmmakers: Hitchcock, Welles, Renoir.*
Writing in the 1930s, Jean Renoir addresses the danger
of technological incursions upon the arts. Yet he also
points out that the school of Impressionism could not
have come into existence without new developments
in technology.

Renoir says that the work of his father, Pierre-
Auguste Renoir the great painter, was made possible—
as well as the creativity of other Impressionists—because
technology in the middle of the nineteenth century had
enabled suppliers to put paints into the little tubes that
we're all familiar with. Until then, they were stored
only in very large jars, and that meant that a painter
was confined to his studio. He couldn't go out into the

streets or the fields with those huge containers. But
with his materials in small tubes, he could easily put
them into a knapsack, range through the countryside,
and paint the landscape. That was the origin of Impressionism. It was an offshoot of technological progress,
which, as we know, can also be perilous in many ways.
There is always this dialectic between destructive
possibility and creative opportunity that the younger
Renoir was very savvy about, and vastly successful in
responding to it throughout film after film.

In his main theoretical writing, *Renoir on Renoir*, he
discusses his own techniques in relation to his art. I
mention his remarks here to emphasize that the possibility of everything going awry because of technology
need not be dismaying. Neither should we be deterred
by the feeling that true love is impossible because of
the inherent difficulties that are even more evident now
than ever as a result of the interpersonal obstacles
imposed by modern life. The all-too-frequent hazards
may have increased, partly because everything changes
very quickly in our day, but we may actually be less
separated, less isolated from each other, than the
pessimists think.

In this regard, consider the affective consequences
that may be caused by the existence of computers.
When you realize how life-enhancing computers are

already, you can imagine how much more beneficial they may become in every way. I remember that when they were first starting to be common—twenty-five years ago, possibly thirty—some of my colleagues said one could tell that students were writing their papers on computers because their literary style had worsened noticeably. That can happen, sometimes it surely does. But I write on the computer, and I don't think my style has deteriorated at all. *I* may have deteriorated. I may no longer be as good a writer as I was, but not because of the computer.

For a number of years now, my first drafts have all been written on a computer. When they are printed out, I write between the lines, and so that stage is largely old-fashioned. The manuscript then goes to a typist, because I can't fluently read my own editing, and it's typed again. The same thing happens over and over, often in more than a dozen drafts. There is thus an intimate relationship between my manuscripts with handwritten editing and the computerized pages that finally issue forth. The writing I do is a joint enterprise between me as someone who grew up to be a writer using a pen or pencil and the computer whose assistance I cherish. It is an extension of myself, even a collaborator, and in any event something I love. I am not fearful that future generations, and their technology-dependent civilizations, will eventually become love-less and unhuman.

On the contrary, there could be in those coming years richer and more loving societies than any that have as yet existed. There may result from future technology new approaches to the nature of love and its ability to transcend the alienation that seemed insurmountable to thinkers like Sartre (or the later Freud). At the same time, the total content of my thought is not overly optimistic. I'm very much concerned about the devious ways in which human beings fail to love. My general doctrine is far from being utopian. What I just said about technology and its possible contributions should not be treated as indubitable assurance. As T. S. Eliot said, between the essence and the descent falls the shadow. In all the areas we have been discussing, we must study and beware of the shadow.

I am sometimes asked whether I think we can ever be able to understand love completely, 100 percent. I usually answer that 100 percent is an arbitrary figure, and that if, as an example of how to approximate it, you introduce the idealized use of artificial intelligence and computational modalities, you will no longer be talking about human beings. I have no way of gauging any such possibility, never having known the perfectible entities being envisaged. I am familiar with

only the carbonized versions that we are, and there is
nothing perfect about us or the nature that we emerge
out of and still inhabit. We are ourselves nature in one
of its local manifestations, and none of that is an
approximation of any perfectibility.

In any event, perfection is not something we ought
to be striving for. Longings of that kind engendered the
fundamental mistakes that Plato made. He was a great
artist who had a highly refined sense of aesthetic goodness, which he expressed in his ideas about absolute
perfection. And, indeed, we can sit and gaze at it, we
can admire it the way a mathematician can relish a
perfect proof in mathematics. But since mathematics is
an abstraction from reality, it cannot reveal how we can
live harmoniously in nature and the world but with no
hopes of certainty.

In itself, love is pervasively bound up with the relationship between the abstract and the concrete. Each
constitutes an extensive portion of what it is to be a
human being. Existing as we do, we fit into both of
those categories. If we contemplate perfections as a
metaphysician might, that activity alone is still a bit of
imperfect reality. The *contents* of what we contemplate
may be a perfection, but only as a play of the mind,
which is always very imperfect, notoriously quixotic
and incomplete, internally diversified like all the rest
of our existence.

I develop this approach in my book *Feeling and Imagination: The Vibrant Flux of Our Existence*. The flux is vibrant because our program includes the pursuit of exhilarating ideals. We live in accordance with multiple idealizations and whatever values that matter to us. We fashion beautiful, even exquisite, conceptions that we generate in our imagination. That is why life can be joyous, especially as it creates the ability to love. For some people the activation of that capacity may permeate much of their experience. Its vibrancy makes life worth living. At the same time, the life that is lived in that manner remains constantly in flux. Having become a *vibrant* flux, however, our existence is neither chaotic nor meaningless. We create meaning in it through those values that imbue life with the vibrancy they engender.

Feeling and Imagination is a sequel to *The Harmony of Nature and Spirit*, which is the third volume of my *Meaning in Life* trilogy. That work is designed to elucidate fundamental questions that eluded my discussions about the nature of love in the previous triad. I argue that the principal mistake of traditional doctrines, particularly religious dogmas, consists of thinking of spirit as being different from nature. The spiritual life, including love as I understand it, is a search for ideals as they *come out* of nature. Spirit is itself a natural facticity, and it is harmonized with nature as a whole to the extent that we are able to appreciate how much of our material being can be transformed through love and related values that we prize. The latter pertain to the life-sustaining goodness of beauty and enlightened morality, which religion can also reflect but which belong most explicitly to an aesthetic capability more deeply engrained in the human species than most traditional religions recognize. Within that setting, I examine in recent books the nature of transformation as related to problems, both affective and cognitive, that pervade not only art forms like film but also reality as we know it.

A climactic chapter in *The Harmony of Nature and Spirit* is entitled "Aesthetic Foundations of Ethics and Religion." In my estimation, religion is neither a falsity nor an ultimate access to absolute truths. It is one way of experiencing the world from within the framework of mythological and sometimes mystical inclinations that many people have. While the classic myths of love are superlative expressions of such affect, all human existence can be seen as potentially, and equally, aesthetic in itself. That was Nietzsche's final message. He thought that the superman was a supreme artist who makes life as a whole into a work of art. My philosophy of love is a complex and detailed analysis in support of this view of his. When philosophers and theologians offer me some transcendental conception of spirit, I shrug my shoulders. I know nothing about that. Like the world itself, love is an emanation grounded in matter, and comparable to its parental origin. It is a dynamic and always changing process. At the same time, it can empower us to live our brief lives with significant fulfillment, sometimes with joy, and often with a sense of residual satisfaction.

Harmonization of Dewey and Santayana

In terms of all this, I wish to mention my ideological indebtedness, not only to the American pragmatism of William James and John Dewey, but also to the non-pragmatistic philosophy of George Santayana. He was a Platonist, or rather Neoplatonist, and I think the greatest in the twentieth century, while also being a materialist and naturalist. The melding of the two perspectives is the crux of his philosophy, and this kind of harmonization of opposites was characteristic of his life and thought in general. He was born a Catholic, but became an atheist at an early age. In his philosophy he argued that science is the only source of truth and that religion is a kind of theological pseudoscience. One of my professors at Harvard called Santayana something that is perceptive and that I have repeated in various places. He said that he was a "Catholic atheist." When I lectured about that a few years ago in Granada, a professor came up to me afterward and remarked, "That's what we all are nowadays in Spain!"

I don't know whether that is true, but when Santayana spoke and wrote as he did, he was attacked by both sides, especially by the religious people. Today the church is more ecumenical and in some aspects more liberal than before. Quite a few of its practitioners may now agree with Santayana. He refused to be listed as a Catholic thinker just before he died, and yet he wrote book after book about Catholicism, about Christianity, about religion, and he understood them better perhaps than almost anyone else. He had a deep comprehension of religious love as well as friendship and other forms of interpersonal human love.

I especially admire Santayana's understanding of a fundamental idea that is native to both types of love. It is the concept of piety. By that he means fidelity to your own beginnings, whatever they may be—your country, the people whom you grew up with, the culture or religion to which you were born. It is a conservative principle that pervades his writings about Catholicism because he himself was immersed in that sensibility even though he could not accept its doctrines as literal truth. He never renounced his initial faith; he just rejected its theistic dogmas. He scorned the beliefs that were incorporated into Christianity by the clerical hierarchy. Now, it would be entirely legitimate to say, as most Catholics do, that you cannot have piety and religious love as a Christian if you do not believe in the incarnation and are, in fact, an atheist. But from an aesthetic point of view, it can make a great deal of sense. And it is from the aesthetic perspective that most of Santayana's philosophy arises—as mine does too, different from Santayana though I am in many details. In my writings I disagree with several of his major ideas about the philosophy of love. At the same time, his basic approach has mattered greatly to me.

As a panoramic statement that is relevant to my work on love and sex, it may be appropriate here to say a little about my own methodology. As I've remarked, I am a maker of distinctions. But these distinctions have a way of leading to other developments, as often happens in the output of a painter or a musician whose later period is a function of previous stages that he or she has gone through and may have digested creatively. Artists sometimes renounce their former work and adopt a newer style or perspective, but somehow the earlier efforts remain present in the subsequent productions. I feel that is true of me. In itself it is coherent with the organic and self-realizationist view of life that

I believe in and try to express in my books. It's one of the things I learned from Dewey. To him this phenomenon alone is the meaning of life, which consists in attaining a harmonious consummation of one's biological as well as social nature as a human being.

That conception underlies what Dewey calls "the continuum of means and ends." You have various ends in anything you do, but to reach them you have to employ a gamut of suitable means. Having functioned successfully, those means become ends themselves, and as such they eventuate in further means, and on and on in a vital flow that is the creation of value in life. As long as the continuum endures and is satisfying to you, particularly if it also contributes to what others care about, you realize your personal potential—it constitutes a good life. The continuum creates the meaningfulness of one's existence and explains what is even signified as either the meaning *of* life or the meaning *in* life. I agree with Dewey about that.

Though Dewey wrote an important book entitled *Art as Experience*, Santayana was a more refined thinker in matters of aesthetics. Santayana was a great stylist and superlative in his literary criticism and its philosophical relevance, whereas Dewey was at his best in presenting a conglomerate of healthy-minded views about how to live and how to engage actively in the world of politics and ethical decision making. My own efforts seek to combine the alternate imaginings of Dewey and Santayana in a dialectic that is meaningful to me. In the course of this personal mission that I seem to have made my life's work, I discovered that Santayana, unlike Dewey or James, said a great deal about love, much more than I had expected. But he did so in a way that was sometimes quite different from what I believed.

In the beginning of my studies, as I remarked in the prefatory note, few reputable philosophers were doing much of anything in this field, and I was cautioned to avoid it because—I was told—I would ruin my career, I would suicidally destroy my professional standing, I would be ostracized by the American Philosophical Association. But I was willing to run that risk, and as the years went by I discovered that my pluralistic approach to love, and my aesthetic view of it, helped me explore new and interesting vistas of life. Moreover, the pursuit of them prevented me from limiting myself to any narrow, artificial, merely analytical tools or definitions, or any pseudoscientific attempts to do philosophy, while allowing me to accept science as a welcome companion in the quest for knowledge and value. By applying my individual experience and perceptions, as any artist would, and then probing how far one could go with whatever distinctions that came to mind, I hoped to stay open to any perspectives that might then arise through the making of fresh distinctions.

If you say to me, "What exactly is your philosophy of love?" I don't have any simple answer. I would reply, Well, there is the distinction I've been proposing between bestowal and appraisal; there is the idea of interdependence rather then dependence—to which I have briefly alluded; there is love as an acceptance of another being; there are different kinds of love—the love of things, the love of persons, the love of ideals; there is the distinction I make in *The Pursuit of Love* among the libidinal, the erotic, and the romantic; and so forth. I analyze the varied types of social, sexual, and religious love in that book, where I also entertain the possibility of a unification among them.

Approaching the love of persons, the love of things, and the love of ideals as I do, I perceive the danger of denigrating any one of them. The love of things, for example, is misconstrued by Santayana. He thinks that ideals—or at least the love of ideals—show forth and possibly constitute the spiritual life, and he writes cogently in that vein. Nevertheless, he doesn't sufficiently emphasize something of equal significance that he may have understood in his private life but did not fully acknowledge in his philosophy. That is the goodness of loving things. Why shouldn't you love things—if you love them properly and don't crave them possessively or allow them to be conducive to an addiction that makes your attachment harmful to yourself as well as others? And, of course, this could happen with the love of persons too. And even with the love of ideals. Think of all the horrible wars that have been fought because people had a love of their ideals that was unswerving, a passion for their elevated principles that was destructive and ultimately ruinous either in itself or in the effect it had on persons who were willing to go out and kill each other for the sake of those ideals. This syndrome has been a constant menace in the history of humanity.

One therefore has to learn how to live with the negative as well as the positive ingredients of some particular form or instance of love. For that reason, I have constantly refused to rank the types of love by means of any a priori hierarchy, or to diminish the value of one or another. I want to fashion pluralistic ideas of what operates in our nature through them all separately and with regard to their feasible coordination. A good life requires an awareness, and acceptance, of that diversified prospect.

The Role of Creativity

There are other explorations that are related to these thoughts and that may take us a little further. I'll mention one that is very strong in my life at the moment. It results from my realization that in trying to make sense out of the rather amorphous concept of bestowal, which has occasioned a great deal of struggle on my part, I continually find there is more that needs to be done. Each time I return to the issue, my thinking seems to have altered a bit. Perhaps this is what I should have anticipated, since I myself keep changing. Nevertheless, I sense a coherence in what I write, and I surmise that the successive explorations may occasionally be enrichments in the vital continuum that my reading of Dewey taught me to seek.

What I am now beginning to appreciate is the fact that bestowal must be treated as a pervasive and imaginative component of human creativity. I dealt with that slightly in *The Harmony of Nature and Spirit,* and then again in *Feeling and Imagination.* But I failed to portray the detailed manner, and extent, to which imagination is related to creativity. I did not establish how greatly the concept of creativity underlies the distinctions I have lumped together as helpful for understanding the nature of love, perhaps because I presented them as one perspective after another without any desire to achieve a grandly unified theory. A solution of that sort—comparable to the computer's answer (42) in *The Hitchhiker's Guide to the Galaxy*—would have been worthless. I didn't want it, and I'm still not interested in it.

Even so, there is an extensive view that I have been skirting, or dealing with obliquely, but now wish to articulate in a straightforward fashion. It addresses the role that creativity plays in all our experience. The issue is central to traditional thinking about love, whether it be God's love, agapē in Christianity, or any form of love among human beings. The search for creativity manifests itself in the desire to love God—as understood by each of the major Western religions as well as others, such as Zen Buddhism and Hinduism—and likewise in most of our theories about the kind of interpersonal love that ordinary people have access to. I find the idea of creativity difficult to work with, but only by striving pluralistically with concepts like it can one truly elucidate what the nature and pursuit of love is. Sex, which is interrelated, of course, I approach in a comparable though still incomplete form in the expanded version of my book *Sex: A Philosophical Primer* and also in *Explorations in Love and Sex*.

In these books I introduce analyses that eluded me in earlier stages of my writing. I try to show how pluralism provides new modes of dealing with both creativity and love. I specifically have in mind my distinction between compassion and sex, or you might say compassion and passionate sex. The distinction I made in *The Goals of Human Sexuality* between "the passionate" and "the sensuous" is relevant here. By sensuous I meant the way in which we enjoy our body, often through contact with some other person. We then gratify ourselves through our senses and for the sake of sensory consummation. The second dimension, the passionate, I described as a powerful need, a strong feeling of ardor or yearning, normally but not necessarily for another person. Sensuous is cool and passionate is not, but they're both aspects of sexuality, unlike one another, though often compatible with each other. When I got to *The Pursuit of Love*, I tried to deploy similar insights about other kinds of love. And then in *Explorations in Love and Sex*, I returned to the original distinction and amplified it within the framework of a distinction between passion and compassion.

The latter of these two I depict as a type of love, since if you feel compassion for another person you bestow value upon him or her in a very special relation that requires its own place within the spectrum of

loving attachments. In studying that niche, I distin-
guished between compassion and pity. This distinction
goes back to Kant, but I conceived of it anew, and with
an awareness of how faulty Rousseau was when he
talked about the two as if they were the same. I treated
compassion not only as different from pity but also
as distinct from the passionate, whether sexual or
otherwise, as well as from the sensuous, which is
limited to enjoyment of one's sense organs.

Compassion interweaves with kindred types of
love—the love of humanity, for example. In some
traditions, Buddhism above all, the divine is envisaged
specifically in terms of compassion. Christianity is more
complex since God acts compassionately in sending
down the personhood of himself that is called his Son.
The Son forgives out of compassion, but it is sinfulness
that elicits his bestowal. In Buddhism compassion
results from the mere existence of suffering, and that
means more to me then any concept of sin. My thoughts
about compassion are therefore closer to those in
Buddhism.

At the same time, my conception attempts to be
inclusive, combining pluralistic views of love, compassion, and sex with the distinction between the passionate
and the sensuous, which may be applicable as well to
sexless interpersonal bonds that are either passionate

or sensuous—or rather the two of them, since most people wish to experience both. In all these matters there is no one simple solution that one should be looking for, or even hoping to come across. Moreover, the issues are further complicated by the fact that, for me at least, all of the acceptable distinctions—for instance, between the sensuous and the passionate—serve to determine not only what love is but also the nature of creativity as a whole.

It was toward that end that I wrote my book *Mozart and Beethoven: The Concept of Love in Their Operas*. In it I examined Beethoven's inspired thinking about the nature of passion, with all the religious overtones in God's giving of himself through the passion of Christ, and likewise the carnal passion embodied in marriage and its preliminaries. Mozart had some insight into the varieties of passion but was generally more concerned about the ramifications of the sensuous.

There are thus different types of creativity, different affective modes that may be approachable through the basic distinction between the sensuous and the passionate. Notice, however, that we are now talking about a distinction between aesthetic elements operating in works of art, musical masterpieces in this case, rather than between a man and a woman or any other pair of living individuals. That alone makes the analysis more intricate, and thus more elusive.

Future Prospects for the Philosophy of Love: Science and Humanistic Studies United

In turning to the nature of creativity itself, I had yet to find—and still continue to search for—some means of progressing along these intellectual branches, these ventures up the tree of the human spirit, and out on one limb or another. In a sense, that is what I have been doing in the present book, by providing these very limited descriptions. For me they all emanate from a vague totality that is my being as the person I am, expressing myself with whatever conceptual piety I can muster toward my life and its past. Still, as Renoir kept saying about his many films, whether any single product is in fact good or bad doesn't matter as much as the artist's ability to keep on doing his work.

I hope I'll be able to. If I can, I would like my further speculations about love to amalgamate some of the research now occurring in neuroscience and in cognitive studies. As in other great American universities, MIT has encouraged the idea of interdisciplinary research between scientists and humanists, philosophers in particular. But thus far little has been achieved in that direction.

At MIT there is quite a large faculty of people in the humanities who are treated with respect by the Institute as a whole. Nevertheless a relative lack of coordinated research exists between them and the scientists. The problem is compounded if we distinguish, as I do, between the humanities and what is humanistic. You can be a practitioner of the humanities and a superior scholar in some branch of them without being humanistic. Epigraphical work in Greek linguistics is part of the humanities, but it isn't especially humanistic, any more than geology is. They both have their rightful role in a university, but to effect the harmonization that is sorely needed at present, given the fact that biological and cognitive studies have advanced so well, one would have to integrate that type of knowledge more overtly, and more intimately, with concerted investigations of an affective sort. And those largely depend upon the humanistic aspects of the humanities.

Poetry, music, literature, theater, film, and other visual arts—all these are thoroughly concerned with human values, emotions, feelings, in short, affect in its entirety that lies beyond the explicit subject matter of the sciences. The humanities can benefit from science, but they suffer badly when reduced to its methodologies, regardless of where the money comes from. Nowadays it often comes from scientific endeavors. There isn't much money in our society at the moment for purely humanistic work. For thirty years brilliant minds have been charging ahead with great success in cognitive and related scientific efforts. But they may now be reaching an impasse that requires a different kind of tactic.

The importance of the humanistic dimension was taken for granted in earlier centuries. And it excelled in creating beautiful love poetry and great works of art based on love and humankind's inspired search for it. Mozart, Stendhal, Verdi, Proust, and many other great artists were not scientific at all. Now we have many great scientists but we're falling behind by not sufficiently including the arts and the humanities, above all in those areas of humanistic thought that could benefit the sciences directly as well as indirectly.

When I first undertook what has become the core of my intellectual life, there wasn't an established profession that I could rely on, since so little was being done by either philosophers or scientists to study the nature of love and sex or the meaning of life, or even the aesthetics of film. The people who counseled me to avoid such flimsy subjects were often very cultivated, but they too were convinced that all investigation along those lines was suspect and surely fruitless. What I've learned is that, regardless of anything I or others have done since then, the need for such work is even greater now than it was before.

The idea is not to put us back into the mindset of the Middle Ages, or even the seventeenth century, or to better appreciate the achievement of St. John of the Cross, for example, a wonderfully imaginative and perceptive poet, or the nineteenth century, where there were brilliant playwrights like Musset and priceless novelists like Stendhal and Jane Austen. The problem is contemporary, so the output must be contemporary. But within the current actuality, there will have to arise new art forms and new branches of science that can deal with many of the unsolved issues that have been placed on the overloaded shoulders of cognitive science and brain or cell research. The latter have borne up under their burdens, but possibly in ways that are less applicable to the problems of ordinary life than if they had been sustained by prolonged cooperation with the humanistic approach in the humanities. That doesn't happen at MIT now, and I don't think it happens anywhere else. Yet the seeds are there.

Index